GOD'S PROPHETIC CLOCK

7 Signs for the End of Days

God's Prophetic Clock: 7 Signs for the End of Days

ISBN: 979-8-89697-986-9

Assembled and Produced for Goose Creek Publishing by
Breakfast for Seven
breakfastforseven.com

Printed in the United States of America.

JOHN HAGEE

Midnight is here. The King is coming.
Are You Ready?

GOD'S PROPHETIC CLOCK

7 Signs for the End of Days

GOOSE CREEK PUBLISHING

CONTENTS

The hands of God's
prophetic clock are
racing toward midnight.

The signs are increasing.
The enemies are aligning.
The birth pangs are intensifying.

The King is coming.
Are you ready?

INTRODUCTION

And they overcame him by the blood of the Lamb, and by the word of their testimony; and they loved not their lives unto the death.

REVELATION 12:11, KJV

On September 10, 2025, at 12:23 MDT, an assassin's bullet pierced the jugular vein of a 31-year-old Christian husband and father, killing him almost instantly.

Of course, I'm referring to Charlie Kirk, a remarkable young man pursuing a calling as a Christian evangelist and Biblical apologist on college and high school campuses. He was also an articulate and passionate advocate for the greatness of both America and Western Civilization.

Kirk correctly understood both to be built on a foundation of Judeo-Christian principles. He knew exactly why Winston Churchill often used the term "Christian

Civilization" to describe the West. He could not separate Biblical Christianity from American greatness and freedom, nor could he have if he'd tried. The two are completely and inseparably connected.

As details about the assassin emerged, it quickly became clear that the young man who pulled the trigger was deluded by the dominant culture into thinking that Charlie Kirk was spreading "hate." Of course, this was completely false. Still, labeling people who openly share Biblical truth as "advocating hate" has been a tactic used by the American Left for several decades.

There is no sugar-coating or spin about the truth of Charlie Kirk's death. He was a Christian man who was murdered in plain sight for confidently making Christian statements in public.

This, dear reader, exemplifies a true martyr. Of course, he wasn't the first. Pagans, driven by demonic forces, have been killing Christians for 2000 years. And my Bible tells me that Charlie won't be the last. In fact, we are approaching a time when many believers will pay the ultimate price for remaining faithful to their Savior. In some parts of the world, this has already begun.

Christian martyrdom rarely makes the news here in the U.S., but hardly a week goes by without believers somewhere in the world being slaughtered just for calling on the name of Jesus.

Here's just a sampling of incidents within a recent twelve-month span of time.

- Between 150 and 200 Christians, including families, children, and the elderly, were killed in a massacre in Benue State, Nigeria.
- Militants killed at least 20 Christian worshipers at St. Elias Church in Damascus.
- Militia troops abducted approximately 70 Christian civilians in North Kivu, DR Congo. They were all beheaded inside a Protestant church.
- Jihadists in Burkina Faso invaded a church during a service and killed 15 worshipers.
- Two masked gunmen opened fire in a church in Istanbul.
- Around 130 Christian worshipers, mostly farmers, were slaughtered in northern Nigeria.

If you haven't heard about any of these atrocities, it's because our dominant legacy news outlets and organizations don't consider any of them worth your attention. It doesn't align with their preferred storylines. Unfortunately, it's become so common lately that some might say it doesn't even qualify as "news."

But if you follow Christian persecution news sources on social media, you know that almost every week features a horrifying incident — one that goes unreported and therefore unnoticed by the wider world.

The numbers tell a sobering story. According to International Christian Concern's 2025 Global Persecution Index, approximately 300 million Christians worldwide now face persecution of all types, including imprisonment, torture, and assassination.[i]

Open Doors' World Watch List reveals that more than 380 million Christians — 1 in 7 believers worldwide — live in nations with high levels of persecution or discrimination.[ii] In 2024 alone, 4,476 Christians were killed for their faith, with Sub-Saharan Africa becoming ground zero for this violence. In 2025, Nigeria was considered the "epicenter" of Christian martyrdom, with over 7,000 slaughtered in the first 7 months.[iii]

Christian persecution has taken on new forms and intensities. In Nicaragua, government hostility toward Christians has escalated dramatically. In India, Hindu nationalism has deprived Christians of their rights through anti-conversion laws and mob violence. Churches have been forced to close across Algeria,

China enforces regulations that criminalize unregistered congregations, and in Afghanistan, the church has been pushed completely underground.

That truth reminds me of the Scripture I mentioned earlier: *"...and they loved not their lives unto the death."*

This brings me back to Charlie Kirk. His assassination shocked America and the world. Tyler Robinson, the 22-year-old shooter, told investigators: "I'd had enough of his hatred. Some hate can't be negotiated out."

But Charlie Kirk's offense was not hatred — it was truth-telling. His offense was not bigotry — it was boldly proclaiming the Word of God in an increasingly hostile culture. His unpardonable sin, in the eyes of an increasingly pagan culture, was standing firmly on Biblical principles against the winds of popular opinion blowing with gale force toward lawlessness and depravity.

For this, he paid the ultimate price.

The murder of Charlie Kirk is more than just the tragic loss of one man, no matter how devastating that loss may be. It acts as a bloody warning flag for you and me—a prophetic signpost showing we have entered the final stage of redemptive history.

As you will see on the following pages, we are on the very brink of a tumultuous, yet thrilling series of events described by ancient writers inspired by the Spirit of

God — such as Daniel, Ezekiel, and the apostle John. And, of course, from the lips of our Savior Himself.

When Jesus spoke to His disciples about the signs of the end, He declared, *"Then they will deliver you up to tribulation and kill you, and you will be hated by all nations for My name's sake"* (Matthew 24:9). Charlie Kirk's assassin and the bloodthirsty militias shooting, hacking, and burning Jesus-followers around the world are just the latest signs of an ancient hatred that has been intensifying at an alarming rate.

But the spirit of antichrist that now stalks the earth has not limited its fury to Christian believers alone. As students of Bible prophecy know, the book of Revelation speaks of a time when both the followers of Jesus and the Jewish people will face unprecedented persecution.

I aim to show how we are witnessing a parallel fulfillment of these prophecies through the alarming rise in global antisemitism. Jew hatred has become not only accepted but even respected in many of the top institutions in the West, especially since the Hamas massacre of October 7, 2023.

The statistics are astonishing. According to a 2025 report by the World Zionist Organization and the Jewish Agency for Israel, antisemitic incidents worldwide have risen by 340% since 2022. In the United States, incidents increased by 288%, while in Canada they rose by an even more alarming 562%.[iv]

Europe has experienced what the European Union Agency for Fundamental Rights calls a "wave of antisemitism,"[v] with France recording nearly 1,600 antisemitic acts in 2024 and Germany seeing 1,383 incidents in Berlin alone.

The Combat Antisemitism Movement documented 6,326 antisemitic incidents globally in 2024 — a staggering 107.7% increase from 2023.[vi] Perhaps most telling, 68.4% of these incidents were linked to far-left ideology, revealing how the spirit of antichrist has infected those who routinely claim to champion tolerance and justice.

This is no coincidence. This is prophecy unfolding before our eyes.

The book of Revelation is not a book of mysteries and riddles designed to confuse God's people. The very word *apocalypse* is rooted in a Greek word meaning "to remove the veil, to uncover, or to make clear."[vii]

As I write these words, God is pulling back the curtain of time and revealing to His Church exactly what is coming and when it will happen. We are not left guessing about tomorrow. Because of the flawless, faithful Word of God, we know exactly what tomorrow holds.

The God of Abraham, Isaac, and Jacob — the God Who keeps Israel and neither slumbers nor sleeps — is the same God Who watches over His Church. He has promised to destroy all nations that come against Jerusalem and the Jewish people. The Almighty has also promised to deliver His bride, the Church, from the wrath to come. Israel and the Church are distinct and separate. They are not interchangeable, and they will not replace each other.

The book of Revelation is not a horror story. It is a drama of victory. It tells of the Church triumphant overcoming death, Hell, and the grave. It describes the rapture of the Church, leaving this broken world for mansions in Heaven.

Satan is a defeated foe. He has been defeated by the Word, the blood, and the name of Jesus Christ. Jesus Christ is the Lion of the tribe of Judah and the Mighty One of Israel, Who is victorious over all.

But until that glorious, soon-coming day when King Jesus returns to rule and reign from Jerusalem, the world will grow increasingly hostile to both Christians and Jews. The assassination of Charlie Kirk is not an isolated incident — it is a harbinger — a warning sign. The rising tide of antisemitism is not just a temporary social problem — it is a prophetic sign. Together, they announce that the time of the end is drawing near.

On the pages that follow, you will find the exact prophetic timeline that guides us from now until the return of Christ. You will learn to recognize the signs Jesus asked us to watch for — signs that are now quickly appearing across the global landscape. You will see how the persecution of God's people, both Christian and Jewish, was predicted long ago and fits into God's prophetic plan. And why these dark days are actually a reason for hope rather than despair.

This book will provide you with Biblical insight to navigate the turbulent times ahead. You'll see how recent events align with ancient prophecies, how the enemies of Israel and the Church are positioning themselves exactly as Scripture predicted, and why America stands at a critical crossroads that will shape its prophetic destiny.

Most importantly, you will find comfort in knowing that our exit from this broken world is very near. The same Jesus Who defeated death on a blood-soaked hill called Calvary is returning — with power and great glory in the clouds of Heaven. He will rule and reign from Jerusalem, and His Kingdom will have no end.

The signs are increasing. The birth pangs are intensifying. The King is coming.

Let's be ready. Read on!

He who testifies to these things says, "Surely I am coming quickly." Amen. Even so, come, Lord Jesus! The grace of our Lord Jesus Christ be with you all. Amen.

REVELATION 22:20-21

CHAPTER 1:

THE COVENANT THAT CANNOT BE BROKEN

Why Israel Is Still God's Chosen Nation

"Can a woman forget her nursing child, and not have compassion on the son of her womb? Surely they may forget, yet I will not forget you [Zion]. See, I have inscribed you on the palms of My hands; your walls are continually before Me."

ISAIAH 49:15-16

On June 6, 1944, as Allied forces prepared for the largest seaborne invasion in history, timing was everything. The success of D-Day hung on every detail being executed right down to the second.

First, the invasion's date had to be carefully chosen. Planners needed calm seas (to allow troop-laden landing vehicles to get across the English Channel); a full moon (to allow navigation without lights for both ships and aircraft); and a low tide (to expose mines near the beaches).

In the early summer of 1944, all of those necessary conditions aligned in a small window on the calendar. That window was June 5–7. Miss it, and the next viable dates were months away — risking a loss of surprise, momentum, and most of all, lives.

After storms scrubbed a June 5 attempt, allied weathermen forecast a possible 24–36-hour break in the storms. Eisenhower polled his commanders at Southwick House before dawn on June 5 and finally gave the "go" order for June 6.

Again, every aspect of the extraordinarily complex, multifaceted plan had to be executed with absolute precision. That is why every one of the hundreds of commanders and leaders involved all set their watches to align — to the second — with a single, super-accurate clock housed at the Royal Observatory in Greenwich, England. To this day, Greenwich Mean Time (GMT) is the standard that sets the correct time in every time zone on earth.

At exactly 6:30 AM, the first wave of Allied soldiers arrived at the beaches of Normandy. They didn't arrive early or late — they arrived precisely when the plan demanded. The invasion's success wasn't just about courage and strategy; it was about knowing the precise moment and being prepared for it.

That clock in Greenwich didn't just measure time — it measured the destiny of the free world.

That clock in Greenwich didn't just measure time — it measured the destiny of the free world.

In much the same way, God operates on perfect time. He has a prophetic clock that has been ticking since the beginning of creation, and at the center of that celestial timepiece stands one nation: Israel. Unlike any human chronometer, God's prophetic clock never loses time, never needs adjustment, and never fails to keep perfect synchronicity with His eternal purposes.

Today, as we watch the hands of God's prophetic clock approach midnight, we must understand not only the season but also the day...the hour...the very minute in which we find ourselves. That requires understanding six critical truths about Israel. The first and most foundational truth is this:

1. Israel Is Not a Political Issue — It's a Bible Issue

Please be clear in your heart and mind concerning this immutable truth: God created Israel. God is the defender of Israel. The Bible says, *"He who keeps Israel shall neither slumber nor sleep"* (Psalm 121:4).

Tragically, the vast majority of Americans, and even many Christians, are unaware of God's tenacious, relentless love for Israel and the Jewish people. That love is a yesterday-today-and-forever love. Why? Because it is covenantal in nature. There are two important groups of people in the Bible: the Jewish people and the Church. If you're wrong about either, your theology is forever flawed, frustrated, and fruitless.

The Jewish people are a covenant people, and the covenants that God made with them still stand. His unconditional covenants with the Jewish people have not been revoked, revised, or replaced by His promises to the Church, as some are teaching today. The Jewish people are a cherished and chosen people. God chose them, and the Bible says they are the apple of God's eye (Zechariah 2:8). In Hebrew the phrase translated "apple of His eye" refers to the pupil — the most sensitive and protected part of the eye.

So, if you start picking a fight with Israel and its people, you are sticking your finger in God's eye. Try sticking your finger in someone's eye and see how quickly you get their attention.

2. Israel — The Only Nation Created by a Sovereign Act of God

What makes Israel different from every other nation on the face of the earth? There are many Biblical reasons. For one thing, all roads of history run through Israel. It is no accident that God's land grant to Abraham, Isaac, Jacob, and their descendants is a strip of land that sits at the intersection of three continents. Everything that is globally important in the past and in the future happens in Israel, and more specifically, Jerusalem.

When Messiah returns, He's not coming to Washington. He's not coming to Boston, Moscow, or

Beijing. He's coming to Jerusalem, Israel. From there, and only from there, He will rule and reign for a thousand years. He's not going to run for office. He's going to rule the world with a rod of iron.

Yes, Israel is the only nation established by a sovereign act of God. The path leading up to that divine act begins in the book of Genesis, which states in its opening words: *"In the beginning God created the heavens and the earth"* (Genesis 1:1). That means God owns the title deed of this planet—it is His. Psalm 24:1 affirms: *"The earth is the LORD's, and all its fullness, the world and those who dwell therein."*

Yes, Israel is the only nation established by a sovereign act of God.

God, as the rightful owner of the earth, entered into a real estate contract with a man named Abraham. God led Abraham to a land called Canaan, pointed to it, and declared, "It's yours. I grant it to you and your descendants in perpetuity." God said:

> *"Also I give to you and your descendants after you the land in which you are a stranger, all*

> *the land of Canaan, as an everlasting possession; and I will be their God."* (Genesis 17:8)

I have to ask: which part of *"everlasting possession"* do Israel's enemies not understand?

Nearly five centuries later, God led several million of Abraham's direct descendants back to the edge of that same land and reaffirmed His previous land grant. This is God speaking to the Israelite tribes:

> *"See, I have set the land before you; go in and possess the land which the* Lord *swore to your fathers — to Abraham, Isaac, and Jacob — to give to them and their descendants after them."* (Deuteronomy 1:8)

When resolving a real estate dispute, you return to the original landowner. In this case, that owner is Jehovah God. If you disagree with the contract, you must address it with Him.

Clearly, the birth of Israel did not take place in 1948 through an act of the United Nations or by a decree of colonial powers. No, Israel was born from an everlasting covenant God made with Abraham in Genesis 12, one of the most pivotal and significant chapters in all of Scripture.

The Bible clearly states that God chose Abraham and his descendants to possess the land of Israel forever. Genesis 13:14–17 says:

> *And the LORD said to Abram, after Lot separated from him: "Lift your eyes now and look from this place where you are — northward, southward, eastward and westward; for all the land which you see I give to you and your descendants forever. And I will make your descendants as the dust of the earth; so that if a man could number the dust of the earth, then your descendants also could be numbered. Arise, walk in the land through its length and its width, for I give it to you."*

I encourage you to write down that verse and refer to it whenever a talking head on television claims the Jews are "occupying" land that isn't theirs. Highlight the phrase *"to you and your descendants forever."*

Recently, many Israel-hating, Jew-hating activists have started using the phrase "From the River to the

Sea, Palestine will be free" as a shorthand for their goal of erasing Israel from the map. They want Arab-Muslim control over all of Israel, from the "river" (the Jordan River on Israel's eastern border) to the "sea" (the Mediterranean Sea on Israel's western border).

But they were not the first to describe this part of the world in such terms. God beat them to it by 4,000 years. In Genesis 15, we see God initiating a "covenant cutting" ceremony with Abraham (more on that soon). You know God means business when a covenant is involved. There is nothing He takes more seriously than His own promises, signed and sealed in blood. After the ceremony, we see this detail and some words from God:

> *On the same day the LORD made a covenant with Abram, saying: "To your descendants I have given this land, from the river of Egypt to the great river, the River Euphrates."* (v. 18)

The "river of Egypt" God refers to here is clearly the Nile. We don't need to guess the identity of the other river either. God makes it clear — "the River Euphrates." Now, look at the current map. Do you see it? The small strip of land that makes up Israel today is much less than what God promised to Abraham and his descendants in His covenant. Still, even that is too much for those who see her very existence as an insult to their warped sensibilities.

3. The Three Types of Biblical Covenants

In the Old Testament, there were three ways a covenant could be finalized: a shoe covenant, a salt covenant, and a blood covenant. I emphasize this because this very issue has nearly sparked a Third World War on multiple occasions in recent years. You need to grasp this concept to properly interpret God's prophetic timeline.

The Shoe Covenant

The God of Abraham, Isaac, and Jacob considers marriage a sacred obligation. It is a holy covenant between a man and a woman, essential for His divine plan to sustain the human race (Genesis 1:28).

God established several safeguards and rules for Israel regarding marriage. Some of these are reflected in the marriage of Ruth and Boaz.

Legal transactions took place at the city gate in front of ten elders. Boaz asked the elders to witness his discussion with Naomi and Ruth's kinsman-redeemer.

Recognizing that redeeming the land would require him to marry Ruth, the kinsman-redeemer relinquished his rights to both and transferred his rights as kinsman-redeemer to Boaz.

To demonstrate that this decision was legal and final, he took off his sandal and handed it to Boaz.

> *Now this was the custom in former times in Israel concerning redeeming and exchanging, to confirm anything: one man took off his sandal and gave it to the other, and this was a confirmation in Israel.* (Ruth 4:7)

Ruth and Boaz married, and their union produced a son named Obed, who ultimately became the grandfather of King David. Twenty-eight generations later, this same union led to Jesus Christ. Consider this: although Ruth was a Gentile, she appears directly in the genealogy of Jesus. This illustrates that even in the Old Testament, Gentiles are connected to the story and destiny of the Jewish people. This is just one example of an ancient covenant or contract.

The Salt Covenant

Although salt is now common and affordable, it was once rare and expensive for most of history. Travelers crossing deserts depended on salt to prevent dehydration. Men often carried a salt pouch for various uses. Its high value meant it was sometimes used as currency to pay workers. The phrase "He's not worth his salt" described a man who was not doing his fair share of work.

In the Bible, salt is used to preserve food, season sacrifices, and establish unbreakable "covenant of salt" agreements. It also symbolizes believers' influence as the "salt of the earth" (Matthew 5:13), emphasizing their preserving influence and distinctiveness in the world. Additionally, salt represents an eternal, incorruptible covenant between God and His people (Numbers 18:19; 2 Chronicles 13:5).

The salt covenant represents an even more binding pact. Here's how it worked: If you and I want to reach an agreement, we verbalize that agreement, and then I take my salt and put it in your pouch. You reciprocate. We shake the salt pouches, mixing the salt grains together, and then shake hands. The agreement is sealed.

The only way to formally break a salt covenant was to retrieve each person's grains of salt and return the other party's salt grains. This was impossible to do, making the salt covenant permanent and irrevocable. However, there is an even more binding type of covenant than this.

However, there is an even more binding type of covenant than this.

The Blood Covenant

The blood covenant represents the most solemn, binding, and severe form of ancient covenant. During the blood covenant ceremony, the parties involved would gather and agree on the terms. They would then kill an animal and divide the carcass in half, creating a pathway between the two pieces.

The two parties then walk together down the path between the pieces, almost like a married couple walking down the center aisle of a church. In doing so, they are symbolically making a sacred vow with their actions. And what is that vow? May whatever has happened to this animal — or even worse — happen to me if I break my promise to this agreement.

As we read, this is precisely the kind of covenant ceremony God made with Abraham in Genesis 15, which He then followed by declaring His divine gift of the land of Canaan to Abraham and his descendants forever.

Yes, the title to the land of Israel was established through a blood covenant in which God Himself was a participant and promissory party. However, the account in Genesis reveals one clear departure from the typical ceremony of that time.

> *Now when the sun was going down, a deep sleep fell upon Abram...*(v. 12)

Let me assure you, it was not customary for one of the parties of a solemn blood covenant to fall asleep before the ceremony even took place. Yet the text here suggests that God Himself put Abraham to sleep. Why? Because God was about to do something in which mere human flesh could play no part.

Reading this in detail, I can't help but think of a previous instance when God caused a man to fall asleep. I'm referring to the time God put a lonely man into a deep sleep in a garden, and that man woke up married.

In Abraham's case, while he slept, God Himself walked between the pieces of the sacrifice in the form of two symbols: a smoking oven and a burning torch. Again, why put Abraham to sleep? Because this was not a contract between Abraham and God. This was God making a holy covenant with Himself.

Because this was not a contract between Abraham and God. This was God making a holy covenant with Himself.

Abraham's only role in this blood covenant was to simply be the grateful beneficiary. Abraham could not break this covenant because he was asleep; however, God bound Himself to His promise to him. So, let me ask you: Do you think God is capable of being unfaithful to Himself? Of course not.

4. The Eternal Nature of God's Promise

God said to Abraham: "I'm going to give you and your seed this land as an eternal covenant forever."

"I'm going to give you and your seed this land as an eternal covenant forever."

Please consider the literal meaning of that word, "forever." It means indefinitely, endlessly, and eternally. "Forever" means forever. It doesn't mean until the United Nations decides to change the rules of the game. No. That property belongs to the Jewish people forever.

In Genesis 17, God, from His throne, decrees the establishment of a covenant with no expiration date:

> *"I will establish My covenant between Me and you and your descendants after you in their generations, for an everlasting covenant, to be God to you and your descendants after you. Also I give to you and your descendants after you the land in which you are a stranger, all the land of Canaan, as an everlasting possession; and I will be their God."* (vv. 7–8)

Please note the phrase *"everlasting possession"* in that final verse. It means right now and always. From Heaven's perspective, the Jewish people rightfully own the land of Israel. They own it today, tomorrow, and forever. It is their land.

The Bible says God is the God Who keeps covenant to a thousand generations (Deuteronomy 7:9). Genesis 15:13–16 very clearly implies that a generation is a hundred years. So, for you literalists, that would mean God's covenant is good for a hundred thousand years, which means it has another 96,000 years to run. And if, for some reason, the earth as we know it still exists after that time, the Almighty would extend His blood covenant with the Jewish people for the land of Israel into infinity.

The Bible says God is the God Who keeps covenant to a thousand generations.

5. The Exclusion of Ishmael

For those genuinely curious about the deed to the Promised Land and the two most famous sons of Abraham — Isaac and Ishmael — please understand that Abraham actually fathered eight sons, not just two. Yes, he had Ishmael through Hagar and Isaac through

Sarah. But the Word of God also tells us that he had six other sons with a servant named Keturah.

In Genesis 17:18, Abraham is negotiating with God, trying to include his "technically firstborn," Ishmael, in the covenant promises God made to him. There Abraham says, *"Oh, that Ishmael might live before You!"* God answered him in the next verse with a single word: *"No."* He then continued, *"Sarah your wife shall bear you a son, and you shall call his name Isaac; I will establish My covenant with him for an everlasting covenant, and with his descendants after him"* (v. 19).

What part of "No" do we not understand? It is Isaac's son, Jacob, and Jacob's twelve sons, the founders of the twelve tribes of Israel, and their line to whom the covenantal promise of the Land belongs.

As for Ishmael, God, in deference to His friend Abraham, said: *"I have blessed him, and will make him fruitful, and will multiply him exceedingly. He shall beget twelve princes, and I will make him a great nation"* (Genesis 17:20). This is indeed a promise from God and like all others, a promise God kept. But it is not a promise that involves the land of Canaan. No, the covenant keys to the land of Israel excluded Ishmael. Which means the Arab nations have no claim to the land of Israel, according to God's legal text — Genesis 17:19–21.

Yet we see that God promised Ishmael, the father of the Arabs, that his descendants would have great wealth and prosperity. He granted this because Abraham loved his son. Today, they are very wealthy, with many Arab states rolling in nearly limitless oil wealth. As it is said, Abraham had two sons: one received the oil, and the other received the land.

Let's conclude this section with a definitive statement of an unchanging truth.

6. God's Foreign Policy in One Statement

The nations of the world have been practicing the art of foreign policy for millennia. Here is God's succinct take on all of it — this is God's foreign policy in one statement:

> *"I will bless those who bless you, and I will curse him who curses you; and in you all the families of the earth shall be blessed."* (Genesis 12:3)

Every man, every nation, every political leader, and every foreign minister must decide: Will we bless Israel, or will we place ourselves under God's judgment? Concerning Israel, this is God's foreign policy.

How many Christians today can explain to a skeptical neighbor God's love for the Jewish people and the unconditional, irrevocable, and irreplaceable blood covenant in Scripture that granted them the land forever? The time has arrived for the Church to realize that Israel isn't just another nation — Israel is God's prophetic clock, and its hands are moving toward midnight.

The covenant cannot be broken because God Himself made it. Abraham was asleep during the ceremony. This was God binding Himself to His own promise. And He is the One Who cannot lie. The One Who keeps covenant for a thousand generations. And as you're about to discover, that covenant revolves around not just a land, but a city.

**God gave Abraham a land.
But at the heart of that land
is a city unlike any other.**

A city God calls His own. A city the whole world is fighting over. A city where the King is coming back.

Jerusalem is not just the epicenter of prophecy. It is the throne of the returning King.

CHAPTER 2:

JERUSALEM – THE CITY THAT GOD CALLS HIS OWN

The Epicenter of Prophecy and the Throne of the Coming King

I have chosen Jerusalem, that my name might be there; and have chosen David to be over my people Israel.

2 CHRONICLES 6:6, KJV

In December 2017, President Donald Trump addressed the nation with an announcement that shocked diplomatic circles worldwide. The United States would officially recognize Jerusalem as Israel's capital and start relocating the American embassy from Tel Aviv to Jerusalem.

The reaction was immediate and completely predictable. Brows furrowed, hands were wrung. There was much wailing and gnashing of teeth among the usual suspects. The United Nations condemned the decision. European allies expressed deep concern. Arab nations erupted in protest. News analysts predicted dire consequences. One headline whined, "Trump Ignores Warnings with 'Reckless Jerusalem Move.'[viii]

A few of those dismayed commentators mentioned that many presidential candidates, dating back to Bill Clinton, promised to do the same during their campaigns. However, none of them followed through on that promise once in office. They also did not note that in 1995, Congress passed the Jerusalem Embassy Act, which authorized and supported such a move.

But President Trump was different. America finally had a president who genuinely meant to keep his promises. Within months, the U.S. embassy opened in Jerusalem — on May 14, 2018 — exactly 70 years after Israel's rebirth as a nation. The move that many said was impossible was accomplished. And contrary to the gloomy predictions, the region did not instantly erupt into war.

Why did this decision matter? Why did simply recognizing Jerusalem as Israel's capital provoke such outrage from the nations? Because Jerusalem is not just any city. Jerusalem is the epicenter of prophecy.

Jerusalem is not just any city. Jerusalem is the epicenter of prophecy.

Jerusalem is the city where God chose to place His name forever. Its walls will hold the throne from which Jesus Christ will someday rule the world. The nations rage because Satan knows these things.

The City Where God Placed His Name

Jerusalem is the only place on earth sacred Scripture calls *"the city of our God"* (Psalm 48:1). It is the plumb line of eternity and the hinge of history. What does that mean? It means you should keep your eyes on Jerusalem, because everything from this point forward in world history is going to start with or involve Jerusalem.

Jerusalem is the hub of this spinning planet. Few Christians realize the supernatural importance of Jerusalem. She is the city of David, the place that God calls home. Jerusalem is where Abraham, the father of all believers, placed his beloved son on an altar on Mount Moriah (now the Temple Mount) and raised the dagger to kill him to demonstrate his trust in God's promises.

Few Christians realize the supernatural importance of Jerusalem.

God stopped him. In that same place, centuries later, God the Father took His Son, the Lamb of God, and placed Him on the altar of the Cross — that you and I could be forever saved and be redeemed by the amazing grace of God.

The Almighty's presence resides in Jerusalem. The Architect of the Universe has clearly stated that He has placed His name there, and His eyes and heart are always focused on the city (1 Kings 9:3; 2 Chronicles 6:6; 7:16).

Jerusalem in Scripture

Yes, God has chosen Jerusalem to be His own. As God states in the verse I cited at the beginning of this chapter: *"I have chosen Jerusalem, that my name might be there; and have chosen David to be over my people Israel"* (2 Chronicles 6:6, KJV).

God has chosen Jerusalem to be His own.

Jerusalem is known as the City of David, the city of the Great King. When you walk through the gates of the Old City, you are walking where David's descendant, Jesus, once walked.

Is there any doubt that Jerusalem is holy to the Lord? The name of Jerusalem appears more than 800 times in the Bible. In the Gospels, Luke 6:45 states, *"For the mouth speaks what the heart is full of"* (NIV). Since God is the Author of the Bible, He has mentioned Jerusalem hundreds of times over thousands of years, reflecting the abundance of His heart. Jerusalem fills God's heart to overflowing.

Similarly, Matthew 6:21 states, *"Where your treasure is, there your heart will be also."* And God has invested a great deal of treasure in Jerusalem. It is the ancestral homeland of the Jews and the place He chose for His only begotten Son to die on a Cross.

Psalm 135:21 says, *"Praise be to the* Lord *from Zion, to him who dwells in Jerusalem"* (NIV). It is the only city where God has set His name, His eyes, and His home. You can be sure that God's heart is where His treasure is.

King David's Love for Jerusalem

King David writes in Psalm 137: *"If I forget you, O Jerusalem, let my right hand forget its skill! If I do not remember you, let my tongue cling to the roof of my mouth — if I do not exalt Jerusalem above my chief joy"* (vv. 5–6).

It seems David couldn't imagine life without Jerusalem. He couldn't envision a world where Jerusalem was forgotten or forsaken. To David, Jerusalem was the very heart of his existence.

In 2 Samuel 5:7, King David conquered Jerusalem. He *"captured the stronghold of Zion, that is, the city of David"* (NASB). And Jerusalem became the capital of Israel. It is in Jerusalem that both the first and second temples were built. It was in Jerusalem that Jesus carried the Cross along the Via Dolorosa in the Old City and paid the penalty of sin on Calvary.

The ground of Jerusalem was stained with Jesus' blood, and one day His nail-pierced feet will touch it again because, when He returns, it will be to Jerusalem.

The ground of Jerusalem was stained with Jesus' blood, and one day His nail-pierced feet will touch it again because, when He returns, it will be to Jerusalem.

The Prophetic Significance of Jerusalem

When Jesus entered Jerusalem for the last time before heading to the Cross, He made a statement that was quite significant about what must happen in this city: *"Jerusalem, Jerusalem, you who kill the prophets and stone those sent to you, how often I have longed to gather your children together, as a hen gathers her chicks under her wings, and you were not willing. Look, your house is left to you desolate. For I tell you, you will not see me again until you say, 'Blessed is he who comes in the name of the Lord'"* (Matthew 23:37–39, NIV).

"Blessed is He who comes in the name of the Lord."

Those verses are important because they give us a clue about what must happen first before Jerusalem sees Jesus again. The key phrase in that passage above pivots when Jesus said, *"Blessed is he who comes in the name of the Lord."*

Jesus will return to earth, and Jerusalem will have an important part in that event. One day, as Revelation tells us, Jesus will come back to the Mount of Olives. Zechariah 14:4 declares: *"In that day His feet will stand on the Mount of Olives, which faces Jerusalem on the east. And the Mount of Olives shall be split in two, from east to west, making a very large valley; half of the mountain shall move toward the north and half of it toward the south."*

A cemetery was established in front of the Golden Gate years ago to try to prevent Jesus from entering through it. The Golden Gate is the only gate around the Old City of Jerusalem that has been walled shut. Every other gate is accessible to pilgrims from around the world, but in a futile attempt to stop the fulfillment of Jesus' prophecy, that gate was sealed. However, one day Jesus will return again and walk through that gate, for nothing can derail the plans and purposes of our great God.

For nothing can derail the plans and purposes of our great God.

The Battle for Jerusalem

The battle for Jerusalem is both physical and spiritual. God Almighty has promised it to His Son, Jesus Christ, to rule the nations during the Millennial Reign. However, Satan is targeting this territory for his son — the Antichrist. This isn't new. Since the fall in Genesis 3, there has been an ongoing struggle for supremacy over this world.

Before Jesus returns, the "man of sin," who is the "son of perdition," will be revealed (2 Thessalonians 2:3). That's the Antichrist. And Satan — that usurper of old — wants his diabolical spawn to rule his global empire from the city of Jerusalem.

This is why the nations rage over Jerusalem. This is why every attempt to divide Jerusalem meets with fierce resistance from Heaven itself. This is why no peace plan that demands Israel give up a single square foot of Jerusalem will ever succeed. God has decreed that Jerusalem belongs to His Son, the King, and no power in Hell or on earth can alter that decree.

God has decreed that Jerusalem belongs to His Son, the King, and no power in Hell or on earth can alter that decree.

God Moves with Stopwatch Precision

As noted in the previous chapter, Israel is God's prophetic clock. This is confirmed by one of the most remarkable prophecies in the Bible. I'm referring to the astonishing and highly accurate prophecy of Daniel about the Persian King Artaxerxes, who issued a decree allowing the Jews to rebuild Jerusalem.

In the ninth chapter of Daniel, we see the angel Gabriel providing Daniel with prophetic insight into the future arrival of the Messiah. This prophecy foretold the passing of 70 prophetic weeks (490 years).

From the time a Persian king authorized the rebuilding of Jerusalem's ruins until the arrival of "Messiah the Prince," 69 weeks (483 years) elapsed, with the final 70th week still in the future. That prophecy proved remarkably accurate.

That prophecy proved remarkably accurate.

The divine prophetic clock for the 483-year period started ticking on March 5, 444 B.C., when Artaxerxes of Persia issued the decree authorizing Nehemiah to rebuild Jerusalem (Nehemiah 2). It would take exactly 173,880 days (483 prophetic years of 360 days each) from that proclamation to the time Jesus rode a donkey into Jerusalem, where he was hailed by the people with "Hosannas" and palm branches (John 12:13). That is, from March 4, 444 B.C., to March 30, 33 A.D.

The accuracy of that prophecy is remarkable. It shows that God Almighty is in control, and everything will happen exactly as He says, how He says, and at the precise time He desires.

Regarding Jerusalem, God acts with stopwatch-like precision. In Psalm 102:13, the psalmist refers to this future fulfillment as a "set time." Writing: *"You (God) will arise and have mercy on Zion; for the time to favor her, yes, the set time, has come."*

The New Jerusalem: Not a Metaphor

Jerusalem is the only city that God promises to make new. In Heaven for eternity, God will dwell in a "new" Jerusalem.

Jerusalem is the only city that God promises to make new. In Heaven for eternity, God will dwell in a "new" Jerusalem.

Revelation 3:12 (ESV) says: *"The one who conquers, I will make him a pillar in the temple of my God. Never shall he go out of it, and I will write on him the name of my God, and the name of the city of my God, the new Jerusalem, which comes down from my God out of heaven, and my own new name."*

In Revelation 21:10, this New Jerusalem is described as the holy city. The apostle John saw it coming down from Heaven, prepared like a bride adorned for her husband.

Let me be absolutely clear: New Jerusalem is not a metaphor. It is not symbolic language. It is not a spiritual allegory. New Jerusalem is a literal, physical city that will descend from Heaven to earth. The Bible describes its dimensions — it is roughly 1,500 miles in length, width, and height. It is a city with foundations of precious stones, gates of pearl, and streets of transparent gold.

New Jerusalem is a literal, physical city that will descend from Heaven to earth.

This is where God's saints will dwell forever. It is the ultimate suburb, the city where roses never fade, where the lame leap with joy, and where the deaf hear and the blind see. It is a city without crying, dying, parting, or sorrow, for the former things have passed away.

It is a city free from death and disease. It is a city where Jesus Christ dwells, for the Lamb is the light of that city. It is the city where Abraham, Isaac, and Jacob reign in mansions built by the Master Architect of ages. It is the city whose builder and maker is God.

The Command to Pray for Jerusalem

As you're beginning to understand, God has a purpose for Jerusalem. He made Jerusalem His own city, and one day He will create a New Jerusalem. It is a holy city because God declared it to be, and it is the city where the tribes of the Lord go up to praise His name (Psalm 122:4–5).

He made Jerusalem His own city, and one day He will create a New Jerusalem.

Considering all this, we shouldn't be surprised to find in God's Word a clear command to pray for Jerusalem's well-being: *"Pray for the peace of Jerusalem."* Psalm 122:6: It is the only city in history to have a direct Biblical command urging believers to pray for its peace.

Here is holy Scripture: *"Pray for the peace of Jerusalem."* That is not a request — that's a king's command. David is not asking you. He's saying, *"Pray."* Therefore, we must do it.

"Pray for the peace of Jerusalem."

We aren't provided with a detailed explanation of why the Bible encourages us to pray for the peace of Jerusalem. However, we do have the exhortation to do so, and that exhortation is followed by a blessing of prosperity and peace. The passage continues: *"May they prosper who love you. Peace be within your walls, prosperity within your palaces"* (vv. 6–7).

After nearly 70 years of walking with God, I've realized that my heart aligns with whoever or whatever I consistently pray for. This holds true for all believers. If you regularly pray for the peace of Jerusalem, your heart will grow to love Jerusalem more. As your heart moves in that direction, you start to love what God loves deeply, and you'll find yourself drawn closer to Him.

Do you desire supernatural prosperity? Pray for the peace of Jerusalem. It will both shake the gates of Hell and open the windows of Heaven. It will make the impossible possible and bring God's blessings that will never end.

Jerusalem: Why It Matters Today

I visited Israel for the first time in 1978. I arrived as a tourist, but I left as an unapologetic Zionist. During that initial, life-changing trip, while praying at the Western Wall, I turned, looked over my shoulder, and saw an elderly Jewish man sitting in a chair, kissing the Torah with tears streaming down his face.

I was deeply moved by this man's passion for the Scriptures and for the God Who delivered them to the Jewish people. In that sacred moment, the Lord spoke to me and said, "That man is your spiritual brother, and you know nothing about him. And he's afraid of you." That encounter at one of Jerusalem's holiest sites changed me and altered the course of my life and ministry.

I realized that the Jewish people as a nation have always been sacred to the Lord, and they always will be. They have endured demonic hatred throughout history — and against incredible odds — they survived because of God's unconditional love for them. If the Spanish Inquisition had wiped them out, or the Eastern European pogroms had destroyed them, or Hitler's "final solution" had succeeded, or Iran and its proxies had achieved their goal to eliminate them, there would be no Israel today.

If there were no Israel, there would be no Jerusalem. And if there were no Jerusalem, then how would Matthew 23:39 and Zechariah 14:4 be fulfilled?

But the Word of God must come true. Heaven and earth will pass away before a single promise or decree of our God fails. All He has decreed will be fulfilled. So, Israel exists. Jerusalem stands. And God's prophetic clock continues to tick toward midnight.

Heaven and earth will pass away before a single promise or decree of our God fails.

When Messiah returns, He's not coming to Washington. The European Union or NATO in Brussels will not have the honor of receiving Him. Nor is He coming to Rome or Russia. No, He's coming to Jerusalem, Israel.

All of this makes what happens in Jerusalem extremely important to us as Christians. Because Jerusalem is not just another city on the map — Jerusalem is the center of all prophecy.

For the same reasons, what occurs in Israel is critically significant to the world.

Yes, the nations rage. The politicians scheme. The United Nations passes its endless, toothless resolutions. Nevertheless, the second psalm tells us that God finds all of this amusing (Psalm 2:1–4).

Throughout its long history, Jerusalem has been destroyed twice, besieged 23 times, attacked 52 times, and captured and recaptured 44 times. Despite its turbulent past, God has plans for Jerusalem. For all eternity, Jerusalem remains the undivided capital of Israel because God Himself wills it. And one day — perhaps very soon — Jesus Christ will return to claim His throne in the city that has always belonged to Him.

For all eternity, Jerusalem remains the undivided capital of Israel because God Himself wills it.

God has always had enemies.
And those enemies have
always had one target.

Israel.

Twenty-six centuries ago,
a prophet named Ezekiel
saw their names. He saw their
alliance. He saw what they would
do — and how they would fail.

The coalition is forming.
The players are on the field.
God is not surprised.

CHAPTER 3:
ISRAEL'S ENEMIES ARE ALIGNING

Gog, Magog, and the Rise of a Prophesied Coalition

"Son of man, set your face against Gog, of the land of Magog, the prince of Rosh, Meshech, and Tubal, and prophesy against him."

EZEKIEL 38:2

On the morning of October 7, 2023, the world watched as roughly 6,000 terrorists breached Israel along the Gaza border at over 100 locations, as well as another 1,000 involved in rocket barrages from within Gaza, ultimately carrying out the deadliest attack on Jewish people since the Holocaust.

In the span of a single day, over 1,200 Israelis and foreign nationals — men, women, children, babies, and the elderly — were murdered in ways that defied human comprehension.

Families were burned alive in their homes. Young people at a music festival were hunted down and slaughtered. Thousands more were injured, and over 250 civilians were dragged into Gaza as hostages. Moreover, human rights organizations accused Hamas of using sexual violence as a weapon of war, later widely proved by survivor accounts.

On that dark day, Hamas terrorists proudly posted videos of it all to social media platforms. Shortly after the attacks, I'd expressed support in a private message to Israeli Prime Minister Benjamin Netanyahu. He wrote a gracious response, part of which included these words:

> *"Israel did not want this war. It was forced upon us by depraved ISIS-like Hamas*

terrorists, with no regard for the sanctity of human life, who have taken root on our borders. However, they miscalculated the strength of our resolve. We will win this war. We will dismantle Hamas."

What the prime minister did not say — but what students of Bible prophecy immediately recognized — was something even more sobering. Namely, that the nations behind that attack were not randomly assembled. They were the exact nations that the prophet Ezekiel identified 2,600 years ago as the coalition that would rise against Israel in the last days. It seems the key players of end-time prophecy are already on the field.

It seems the key players of end-time prophecy are already on the field.

The Prophecy Hidden in Plain Sight

As I write this book, America, led by President Donald Trump, and Israel, led by Prime Minister Benjamin Netanyahu, launched Operation Epic Fury and

Operation Roaring Lion, respectively, in response to Iran's imminent nuclear threat. Over 40 of Iran's top leaders were eliminated by Israeli airstrikes. Now, the world watches as they wait to see if the Iranian people will rise to reclaim their nation from the ruling despots.

Now, the world watches as they wait to see if the Iranian people will rise to reclaim their nation from the ruling despots.

If you want to understand the headlines coming out of the Middle East, don't start with cable news or social media. Begin with Ezekiel 38 and 39. The prophet Ezekiel wrote these words while in Babylonian captivity, under Nebuchadnezzar's rule. God sent him to the Jewish people in Babylon (modern-day Iraq), where they had been for several hundred years, to remind them that God's purpose for them was not permanent slavery but an eventual return to their Promised Land.

But God also granted Ezekiel a vision that reached far beyond his own lifetime. He revealed to him a coalition of nations that would arise in "the latter days" and come against Israel like a storm. Look with fresh eyes at Ezekiel 38:15–16:

> *"Then you will come from your place out of the far north, you and many peoples with you, all of them riding on horses, a great company and a mighty army. You will come up against My people Israel like a cloud, to cover the land. It will be in the latter days that I will bring you against My land, so that the nations may know Me, when I am hallowed in you, O Gog, before their eyes."*

Notice that phrase: *"the latter days."* In prophetic terms, that means after Israel is reborn as a nation. We've been living in the latter days since 1948. God is speaking directly to Russia in this passage. How do we know this? Keep reading.

Russia: The King of the North

Bible prophecy describes several powerful alliances engaged in a future global, multi-sided battle leading up to Christ's second coming. These groups are positioned geographically in relation to the holy city of

Jerusalem. From God's perspective, Jerusalem is the center of the universe.

From God's perspective, Jerusalem is the center of the universe.

Prophetic events in the last days focus on four kings: the King of the North, the King of the South, the King of the East, and the King of the West.

1. The King of the North mainly refers to Russia or Rosh. (Daniel 11; Ezekiel 38–39).
2. The Kings of the East are described as a coalition consisting of forces from the Orient and the Far East, beyond the Euphrates River. (Revelation 16:12).
3. The King of the West is made up of the Western powers within the revived Roman Empire, a European alliance led by the Antichrist, who is described as the "little horn" of Daniel 7 and the "beast" of Revelation 13.
4. The King of the South is composed of an Egyptian Arab alliance from the Ptolemaic dynasty, established by Ptolemy I after Alexander the Great's

death. Egypt will lead the African forces in the struggle for control of a world empire. (Daniel 11)

Gog and Magog

Ezekiel 38:2:

> *"Son of man, set your face against Gog, of the land of Magog, the prince of Rosh, Meshech, and Tubal, and prophesy against him."*

Gog is a man; Magog is a kingdom. The word translated here as "Rosh" is a proper name related to the same linguistic roots as the name "Russia." Similarly, Meshech linguistically points to Moscow. And Tubal refers to Tobolsk, a Russian city. (Ezekiel 38, 39)

The Hook in the Jaw

In Ezekiel 38:4, God speaks to the nations that will come against Israel from the north: *"I will turn you around, put hooks in your jaws and bring you out with your whole army"* (NIV).

What hook is God going to use to pull those nations into the Middle East? I believe that hook is oil.

Oil controls the global economy. It is an essential component for all superpowers. If you don't believe the world economy is driven by oil, you haven't been paying attention to recent geopolitical events. Consider this: in less than 60 days, the United States and Israel significantly disrupted two of the top illicit sources of oil (Venezuela and Iran) for China.

Oil controls the global economy. It is an essential component for all superpowers.

The Coalition Revealed

Now, examine the allies that will march with Russia against Israel. Ezekiel clearly lists them in verses 5 and 6: *"Persia, Ethiopia, and Libya are with them, all of them with shield and helmet; Gomer and all its troops; the house of Togarmah from the far north and all its troops — many people are with you."*

Let me explain: Persia is, of course, modern-day Iran. The same nation that continued developing nuclear weapons even after the U.S. B-2 strikes in June 2025 during Operation Midnight Hammer. It is the same nation that calls America the Great Satan and Israel the Little Satan. It is the same nation that has repeatedly sworn to wipe Israel off the map. It is the same nation that has killed American citizens and service members worldwide for nearly half a century, starting with the 1979 Islamic Revolution and the subsequent U.S. Embassy hostage crisis. It is the same nation that funds and operates through its own forces (IRGC) and proxy militias (groups in Iraq, the Houthis, Hezbollah, and Hamas) that carried out the October 7 attacks on Israel, which included the deaths of 46 Americans.

Ethiopia represents the Islamic Arab Spring countries — basically, the parts of Africa influenced by Islam. Remember when commentators years ago praised "the Arab Spring" as a new kind of democracy? How did that turn out? Egypt, Libya, Somalia, and several other countries are likely to be part of this coalition.

Germany is Gomer. While Germany remains a strong ally of Israel, 2025 experienced increased tension as Chancellor Merz paused some weapons deliveries and criticized Israeli policies in the West Bank and Gaza.

Togarmah is present-day Turkey. For many years, Turkey was a secular, Western-leaning country working to modernize. Recently, President Recep Erdoğan has been guiding the country toward an Islamic theocratic dictatorship. As he has done this, the attitude toward Israel has grown increasingly hostile.

The attitude toward Israel has grown increasingly hostile.

Recently, Erdoğan has personally criticized Israeli Prime Minister Benjamin Netanyahu, calling him the "butcher of Gaza" and comparing him to Adolf Hitler. Turkey has repeatedly refused to categorize Hamas as a terrorist organization. Instead, Erdoğan's Turkey regards Hamas as a "liberation movement" and often hosts high-ranking Hamas officials.

In November 2024, President Erdoğan announced that the Turkish government had cut all diplomatic, trade, and military ties with Israel because of the ongoing war in Gaza. In November 2025, Turkey issued arrest warrants for Netanyahu and other senior Israeli officials, accusing them of "genocide and crimes against humanity."

It doesn't require much imagination to picture Turkey (Togarmah) joining Ezekiel's coalition of nations against Israel. But who is the leader of this group of Israel-hating states? Look at verse 7: *"Prepare yourself and be ready, you and all your companies that are gathered about you; and be a guard for them."*

The word "guard" in this verse means leader or commander. Russia is the leader of this coming Islamic coalition. Since 2022, Russia has been demonstrating its strength. Following their February 2022 invasion, Russia has occupied large parts of Ukraine, officially claiming to annex four regions — Donetsk, Kherson, Luhansk, and Zaporizhzhia. As of early 2026, Russia continues to control about 20% of Ukraine's territory.

Russia is the leader of this coming Islamic coalition.

Russia and Iran: The Unholy Alliance

Let me connect the dots with rock-solid facts. Iran receives economic, military, and diplomatic support from Russia. The two countries are strengthening their strategic alliance, highlighted by a 20-year deal signed in early 2025. Key support includes supplying advanced aircraft like Mi-28 helicopters and Su-35 fighters, aiding Iran's missile programs, and helping with its surveillance technology.

Their alliance aims to bypass Western sanctions and expand regional influence. Iran, with Russia's support, has been arming and training Israel's enemies for decades. Hamas in Gaza and Hezbollah in Lebanon are just two of Iran's proxies, which, in turn, serve as proxies for Russia.

Now, when you think of a terrorist group, you might picture a small group of people in ragged clothing hiding in caves. That does not describe Hamas and Hezbollah. Before Israel significantly reduced their capabilities after the October 7th attack, both groups were well-funded and armed. They also had highly trained, well-equipped military units. If they don't wear uniforms, it's only to blend in with civilians so they can use school children and hospital patients as human shields.

Indeed, many senior leaders of Hamas and Hezbollah have become billionaires in recent years as they siphoned off international aid money and stored it in accounts in Qatar, Dubai, and Switzerland. A 2023 news report estimated the net worth of Hamas' top three leaders at about $11 billion. That is "B" for BILLION!

All the while, Russia (the "King of the North") and China (the "King of the East") stand back, pretending to be innocent bystanders. They are not. Russia and

China have acted as Iran's main protectors. Whenever concerns arise about Iran's funding and training of terrorist organizations or about its nuclear program, Russia and China rush in to ensure that meaningful international action will be minimized.

There is no regime, dictator, or terrorist organization on the planet so vile, despicable, or repressive that Russia, China, and Iran — working together — won't support to achieve their goal of world dominance. Please note that all three were deeply involved in the corrupt Maduro narco-terror regime in Venezuela that was disrupted in January of 2026 by the Trump Administration.

There is no regime, dictator, or terrorist organization on the planet so vile, despicable, or repressive that Russia, China, and Iran — working together — won't support to achieve their goal of world dominance.

But for Russia, Israel is a unique investment — the ultimate prize and the key to controlling the Middle East. Vladimir Putin does everything he can to strengthen Iran's economy and support the oppressive, repressive dictatorship of the Ayatollah, including selling them weapons and helping develop Iran's nuclear missile program. While Russia and China don't agree on everything, they agree on pushing back against America's presence in the Middle East, directly challenging America's ability to defend Israel.

Consider how the American economy is increasingly at China's mercy. And by constantly posing a growing threat to peace and stability in the Pacific, China has the ability to weaken any U.S. administration's capacity to support Israel.

Israel Surrounded

History shows us that few things are more dangerous than a despot intent on building an empire. And this is what Israel is currently confronting:

- Putin is bent on rebuilding and restoring the former Soviet empire.
- Mullahs of Iran are committed to exporting their Islamist revolution far beyond the borders of Persia.

- Erdoğan in Turkey talks about restoring the former glory of the Ottoman Empire.

Bottom line, Israel is like an island surrounded by aggressive, ambitious "kings" eager to expand their empires. These "kings" aren't going anywhere. Their ambitions are as voracious as ever. In other words, we're not waiting for some mysterious something to happen before we can say, "Everything's ready."

Bottom line, Israel is like an island surrounded by aggressive, ambitious "kings" eager to expand their empires.

The God Who Keeps Israel

The message of Ezekiel 38 and 39 is this: An Islamic horde led by Russia will attack Israel in an attempt to erase Israel from the map and the Jewish people from the face of the earth. But there is good news in these prophecies. They will fail.

Why? Because the Defender of Israel — the God of Abraham, Isaac, and Jacob — the God Who made an unconditional and everlasting covenant with Abraham four thousand years ago (as we explored back in Chapter 1) — promises that He will personally intervene on behalf of besieged, little Israel.

In Ezekiel 38:18, God says, paraphrasing: *"I'm going to show up, and you're going to see fury in My face. I am going to step in and wipe these conspiring attackers out because I am the Defender of Israel."*

These remarkable, prophetic chapters in Ezekiel not only show us that God will supernaturally intervene to destroy these invading armies but also reveal how He will do it.

God's Threefold Judgment

First, God will use a massive earthquake to open the ground and swallow a significant portion of the invading force. He has done this before. When Moses faced opposition from Korah and his followers, God told him to assemble the dissenters at the tent of meeting. The ground opened, swallowed them alive, and then closed over them. That is precisely what will happen to part of this invading army. God will literally bring the mountains down on them (Ezekiel 38:19–20).

Second, chaos will break out among the nine armies. Nine armies speaking nine different languages will gather on the small piece of land called Israel. The Bible says everyone's sword will be turned against his brother (Ezekiel 38:21). In modern terms, it will be a catastrophic "friendly fire" incident on a large scale. Confusion will take over as joint forces turn on each other.

Confusion will take over as joint forces turn on each other.

Once again, there is ample Old Testament precedent for this. It occurred with the Midianites in Judges chapter seven. It happened to the Philistines in 1 Samuel chapter fourteen. And it took place with the Ammonite-Moabite Alliance in 2 Chronicles chapter twenty.

In each case, pagan armies faced God's people with overwhelming force and numbers. And in each case, God caused confusion among them, and they turned on each other — leading to their complete destruction.

Third, God will rain down hailstones, rain, and brimstone from Heaven. Ezekiel 38:22 states:

> *"I will rain down on him, on his troops, and on the many peoples who are with him, flooding rain, great hailstones, fire, and brimstone."*

In the Old Testament, stoning was the punishment for violating God's law. Here, God directly and personally stones the armies of these "kings" who dare to defy Him.

Through these three acts, God declares to the nations that He remains Israel's Protector, still sovereign, and still holds all power in Heaven and on earth. No nation or coalition of nations will succeed against Israel.

Five Out of Six

Here's something remarkable. In the King James translation of Ezekiel 39:2, we read: *"And I will turn thee back, and leave but the sixth part of thee."* That means five out of six soldiers in this massive coalition army will be killed. Five-sixths of the Russian and Islamic forces — destroyed.

Why does God leave a sixth? He wants to leave witnesses to His power. He spares messengers who will return and say, "We went down to Israel in the name of our God, and we got destroyed. God Almighty wiped us out. We don't have an army anymore."

In these two yet-to-be-fulfilled prophetic chapters, we observe a future day when the King of the North and the King of the South will be defeated. Both will be wiped from history forever.

What Happens Before the Storm

I believe, based on God's Word, that when the final battle in the Middle East ends, and the last shot is fired, the flag of Israel will still fly above the ancient walls of Jerusalem. Russia will be defeated, Iran will be defeated, and the radical Islamic nations that attack Israel will also be defeated.

Russia will be defeated, Iran will be defeated, and the radical Islamic nations that attack Israel will also be defeated.

But what will happen before that final conflict? The Bible clearly tells us. The Church of Jesus Christ will be taken from the earth in the twinkling of an eye.

> *For the Lord Himself will descend from heaven with a shout, with the voice of an archangel, and with the trumpet of God. And the dead in Christ will rise first. Then we who are alive and remain shall be caught up together with them in the clouds to meet the Lord in the air. And thus we shall always be with the Lord.*
> (1 Thessalonians 4:16–17)

These events should matter to us, and we need to understand their significance. We're not merely bystanders witnessing distant events that don't affect us. If it involves the God of Abraham, Isaac, and Jacob and His covenant nation, then it involves every believer.

The enemies of Israel are aligning exactly as Ezekiel said they would. The coalition is forming. The hooks are in the jaw. The players are on the field. And Jesus, the One Who *"keeps Israel shall neither slumber nor sleep"* (Psalm 121:4), is coming for His Church.

Every nation faces a choice. Every nation makes a decision. And every nation lives — or dies — by the consequences.

History is a boneyard of empires that chose wrong.

Now it is America's turn. Bless Israel and be blessed. Curse Israel and face judgment. The choice before this nation could not be clearer.

CHAPTER 4:

AMERICA AT THE CROSSROADS OF PROPHECY

Blessing Israel or Facing Judgment

"I will bless those who bless you, and I will curse him who curses you; and in you all the families of the earth shall be blessed."

GENESIS 12:3

In 1492, the same year Christopher Columbus set sail for the New World, Spain carried out one of the greatest acts of national self-destruction in history. In a self-inflicted wound for the ages, King Ferdinand and Queen Isabella issued the Alhambra Decree, ordering all Jews to convert to Catholicism or leave Spanish territory within four months. About 200,000 Jews were expelled, and Spain deliberately abandoned a population that had contributed greatly to its culture, commerce, and intellectual life for centuries.

Columbus himself set sail from Palos de la Frontera on August 3, 1492—just one day after the final deadline for Jewish expulsion. Records indicate that some key members of Columbus's crew had Jewish ancestry, and some historians believe Columbus may have had Jewish blood himself. The ships that would discover a New World left a kingdom that had just banished God's ancient people.

What followed for Spain is a case study in the long-term consequences of cursing Israel. Within a century, the mighty Spanish Empire — the strongest nation on Earth — began its slow, steady decline. The Spanish Armada, Spain's main navy fleet, was destroyed in 1588 during an attack on England.

The British fleet routed the Spanish navy, forcing it to retreat in flames. Then a fierce storm finished the destruction. More Spanish sailors died from drowning and starvation than from combat with the British. A battered remnant of what was once the greatest naval force ever assembled limped back to Spain in shame.

The gold and silver extracted from the Americas led to internal corruption instead of long-term prosperity. By the twentieth century, Spain had become a neglected corner of Europe, divested of its colonies, devastated by civil war, and diminished from its former splendor.

The gold and silver extracted from the Americas led to internal corruption instead of long-term prosperity.

Time and again, this refrain echoes throughout history. The power of the Spanish Inquisitors has fallen. The might of the Third Reich has been diminished to nothing and thrown into the dustbin. Indeed, every nation, empire, and army that has fought against the Jews, even if they appeared to succeed for a time, is now insignificant. Why? It's simple. The Jews belong to

God, and He has vowed to confront those individuals or nations that oppose His beloved.

Today, America faces the same crossroads that other great nations have faced. The question before us is clear and unavoidable: Will we bless Israel, or will we find ourselves under God's judgment? The answer to that question will shape America's future more decisively than any election, economic policy, or military alliance.

Today, America faces the same crossroads that other great nations have faced.

To truly value this pivotal moment for our country, it is wise to review the cautionary stories of other great, powerful nations that faced similar choices and made poor decisions.

The Graveyard of Empires That Cursed Israel

It stands as a Biblical principle confirmed repeatedly throughout redemptive history: what you do to Israel and the Jewish people, God will respond in kind.

This is not an allegory. It is not a metaphor. It is a divine promise and a historical fact that has played out across the ages with remarkable consistency.

It is a divine promise and a historical fact that has played out across the ages with remarkable consistency.

Pharaoh drowned the male Jewish children. The result? God drowned Pharaoh and his army in the Red Sea. The Egyptians enslaved the Jews, aiming to deprive them of any economic benefits and keep them impoverished. But after ten plagues—destroying their crops, killing their cattle, slaying their firstborn males, and drowning their army—the Egyptians happily surrendered all their gold and silver to God's people just to get them to leave. One of the wealthiest nations of its time became poor overnight.

Where are the Persians who threatened to hang the Jews? Gone. Where are the Babylonians? Gone. Where are the Greeks? Gone. Where is the Ottoman Empire? Gone. Where is the Roman Empire that crucified Jesus Christ? Gone. Where are those goose-stepping Nazis and Adolf Hitler? They are all footnotes in the boneyard of human history.

But where is Israel? Israel lives! Israel prospers and thrives. It is a mighty nation blessed by God (Genesis 12:3). The Jewish people remain the apple of God's eye (Zechariah 2:8). They continue to be the people of His covenant (Romans 11:28–29). They are still a chosen people (Deuteronomy 7:6). They remain the cherished people (Jeremiah 31:3).

Forever and always, God Almighty is the Defender of Israel. The nations of the earth that have sought to bless Israel have been blessed, while those that have sought to destroy Israel have faded from history. This is not a coincidence; it is a covenant.

Forever and always, God Almighty is the Defender of Israel.

As I explained in Chapter 1, God made an unbreakable blood covenant with Abraham — one in which Abraham was asleep during the ceremony, making it impossible for human faithlessness to void it.

Today, the Jewish people live in their ancestral homeland, speaking and studying the Torah in Hebrew.

Additionally, the Biblical Feasts of the Lord are once again celebrated in Israel, just as they were thousands of years ago, in the very same land.

Israel as a nation stands as a sign and a wonder to the world that everything they've been through as a people has not weakened them. They continue to grow stronger because God has made it clear: Israel is His land, Jerusalem is His city, and He gave both to the Jewish people. All of this brings me home — to my country — and to those crossroads I previously mentioned.

Israel is His land, Jerusalem is His city, and He gave both to the Jewish people.

America's Dangerous Flirtation with Judgment

Remember God's foreign policy from Chapter 1? *"I will bless those who bless you, Israel, and those who curse you, I will curse."* That is His unchangeable, eternal stance. The question is: which side of that timeless equation will America choose? That's an honest question, and it deserves an honest answer.

The question is: which side of that timeless equation will America choose?

Elections matter. A few years back, America made a series of disastrous foreign policy choices concerning Israel and its enemies. However, more recently, that trend has turned around. Consider the facts:

America, through several previous administrations, sent billions of dollars to Iran — the world's leading sponsor of terrorism. Where did Iran get the money to finance Hamas' construction of more than 300 miles of tunnels beneath hospitals, schools, and apartment complexes in Gaza? These tunnels cost billions. Iran supplied that money. And where did Iran get it? American presidents provided it to them.

We've had political leaders who pressured Israel to make concessions with terrorists; who withheld weapons from our only true ally in the region while they were fighting for survival; and who threatened to cut off support unless Israel accepted burdensome, even deadly conditions. Those leaders were not pursuing a wise foreign policy. In fact, they were risking the judgment of Almighty God.

I thank God that Israel recently gained a strong ally in the White House. That change has made a big difference. As I said, elections matter. Here's why.

When America Has Blessed Israel

God's foreign policy declaration works both ways. When America blesses Israel, America is blessed. At the start of Chapter 2, I mentioned President Trump's decision to relocate the U.S. embassy from Tel Aviv to Jerusalem. That was a supernatural fulfillment of prophecy and a significant moment in Israel's history, in which I played a small part.

God's foreign policy declaration works both ways. When America blesses Israel, America is blessed.

I vividly recall the day America's ambassador to Israel, David Friedman, called and asked if I would come to Jerusalem to pray at the dedication ceremony marking the opening of our embassy there. Naturally, I was humbled and honored to have that opportunity. Why me?

Some months earlier, my wife Diana and I attended a White House dinner, where I took the opportunity to encourage the 45th President of the United States to fulfill America's long-neglected promise to move its embassy to Jerusalem. I pointed out that the ideal date for such a move was approaching.

Namely, Israel's 70th anniversary as a nation-state occurred on May 14, 2018. At the end of our conversation, the president said he would follow through. And as history shows, despite protests and strong resistance, he did exactly what he promised.

And as history shows, despite protests and strong resistance, he did exactly what he promised.

It is hard to fully grasp the spiritual and natural significance of that single act. What I'm saying is this: when you start blessing Israel, God pours out blessings on your life faster than you can receive them. This principle applies to individuals, churches, and nations.

The time to favor Zion is now, and America must decide which side of history — and more importantly, which side of God's judgment — we want to stand on.

Despite the historic embassy move and our recent international support for Israel's right to respond to the horrific attack on October 7, 2023, as well as our involvement in Operation Midnight Hammer and Operation Epic Fury, I still have good reasons to be concerned about the question.

There is a set time in God's prophetic calendar. That time is now.

The Rise of Antisemitism in America

Jew hatred has surged since the devastating 2023 attacks on Israel. The numbers are alarming. In 2024, the Anti-Defamation League recorded 9,354 antisemitic incidents nationwide — and 58 percent of those were also linked to hatred of Israel.[ix] In New York City alone during 2025, police documented 330 antisemitic hate crimes, making up 57 percent of all hate crimes in the city.[x] But the cold, hard statistics only reveal part of the story.

But the cold, hard statistics only reveal part of the story.

In May 2025, a gunman fatally shot two Israeli Embassy staff outside a Jewish community event in Washington, D.C., shouting "Free Palestine" while in custody. Federal prosecutors charged him with two counts of first-degree murder.[xi]

In June 2025, a man attacked attendees at a hostage-awareness event in Boulder, Colorado, using incendiary devices and making pro-Palestinian statements. An 82-year-old woman died 24 days later from her injuries.[xii] That same month, authorities in San Antonio prevented a planned mass shooting at a Jewish community center.[xiii]

On October 7, 2025 — the anniversary of the Hamas massacre — a Minneapolis synagogue was vandalized with threatening messages, including "Watch out Zionists" and references to "Al-Aqsa Flood."

And although it did not happen on our shores, in December 2025, two terrorists opened fire at a Chanukah celebration at Bondi Beach in Sydney, Australia, where 15 people were killed, and 40 were injured — the largest massacre of Jews since October 7th, 2023.[xiv]

In January 2026, Mississippi's first synagogue was severely damaged by a fire determined to be arson. Two treasured Torah scrolls were completely destroyed in the library, and five others in the sanctuary were damaged. Miraculously, a historic Torah that survived the Holocaust remained undamaged.[xv]

This is America today. This is the new normal. On college campuses nationwide, visibly Jewish students live, study, and worship in fear.

This is America today. This is the new normal.

Who could have ever imagined that in America, we would witness the day when hundreds of Ivy League students storm campus streets shouting antisemitic phrases like "From the river to the sea, Palestine will be free"? The Wall Street Journal published a survey conducted by UC Berkeley professor Ron Hassner, who polled 250 university students shouting that phrase.[xvi]

Only 47 percent could identify the river or the sea. Others believed "the sea" referred to the Dead Sea. More than 10 percent thought Yasser Arafat was Israel's first prime minister. These are supposed to be America's "best and brightest."

It's easy to roll one's eyes at how uninformed and misinformed the average American college student or college professor is these days. Yet how many American

Christians can clearly explain God's love for the Jewish people to someone curious? How many can describe how God used a blood covenant to give the Jews the land of Canaan forever? The ignorance cuts both ways. Most Americans and even most Christians remain unaware of God's love for Israel and the Jewish people — yesterday, today, and forever.

Most Americans and even most Christians remain unaware of God's love for Israel and the Jewish people — yesterday, today, and forever.

Antisemitism is a sin, and by its very nature, it damns the soul. Antisemitism on American college and university campuses — and now spilling into our streets, community centers, and many of our churches, as well as so-called Christian social media influencers — can only invite God's judgment on this nation if the rising tide is not stopped.

Jesus said in Matthew 25:40, *"Inasmuch as you did it to one of the least of these My brethren, you did it to Me."* The "My brethren" there is not us. Jesus never called Gentiles His brethren. He's talking about the Jewish people.

> ***"Inasmuch as you did it to one of the least of these My brethren, you did it to Me."***

One of the things the Bible clearly states is that accepting good and not showing appreciation for it is like returning evil for good. I'm concerned that many Gentiles have brought a curse upon themselves because they have received good from the Jewish people and have responded with evil. If you're harboring antisemitism in your heart, I urge you, for your own good, to purge it.

God Is Watching Washington

The truth is clear: God will judge or reward us based on how we treat Israel and the Jewish people. Are you paying attention, Washington? Senators?

Congressmen? There is a God Who observes everything, even the deepest thoughts of the heart. Be aware.

There is a God Who observes everything, even the deepest thoughts of the heart.

God is watching all the time. The Bible states that His eyes are on Jerusalem day and night. May our leaders take note of the sobering declaration of Psalm 33:10–12:

> *The LORD brings the counsel of the nations to nothing; He makes the plans of the peoples of no effect. The counsel of the LORD stands forever, the plans of His heart to all generations. Blessed is the nation whose God is the LORD, the people He has chosen as His own inheritance.*

What does that mean? It means God could not care less about the opinions of a Senate subcommittee, the Kremlin, the United Nations, or anyone else when it comes to Israel. The nations don't matter to God. Their counsel is useless. Their plans have no effect.

Only the counsel of the Lord endures forever. And He has spoken.

Our nation right now, in a day when Israel is fighting for its life, must not, as leverage, threaten to abandon the State of Israel, as has happened repeatedly in the past. We need to wake up as a nation and continue to elect leadership that will lead us back to being an America that stands resolutely on the side of God. God's wonderful promise must not be forgotten: *"I will bless those who bless you."*

God's wonderful promise must not be forgotten: *"I will bless those who bless you."*

A Warning from History

Decades ago, before the collapse of the Soviet Union, I had an encounter that gave me the opportunity to share God's blessing-and-cursing principle in a powerful way. I was ministering in Berlin, Germany, where I visited the Berlin Wall.

A young German woman who was attending our meetings approached me, her face full of concern. She asked, "Pastor Hagee, why did God allow the Communists to build a fence around the German people?"

I looked at her and said, "Because your mothers and fathers built a fence around the Jewish people. They did it at Auschwitz-Birkenau. They did it at Dachau, Buchenwald, Mauthausen, Majdanek, and hundreds of other concentration camps. And they did it with the intent to eliminate the Jewish people." I continued, "God positioned the machine gun towers because that's what your parents built to target the Jewish people who tried to escape. They have German Shepherd dogs guarding you because that's what your parents did to the Jewish people. God has it down to the dog hair. Exactly what you did to the Jews, God is allowing it to happen to you."

She gasped for air and said, "I never thought about such a thing." I responded, "It's the law of God, and it's something the nations of the world must learn." What about America? If we do not continue to stand with Israel and stop the Jew hatred that has infiltrated our nation, God will not continue to stand with America. It's really no more complicated than that.

Compromise Is Rebellion

Considering all the reasons I've mentioned so far, we must conclude that political compromise with Israel's enemies is a form of rebellion against God. Backroom deals with nations that have sworn to destroy Israel are not diplomacy; they are deception and betrayal. Such agreements will not create peace but will only ensure war.

Considering all the reasons I've mentioned so far, we must conclude that political compromise with Israel's enemies is a form of rebellion against God.

Islamic imams teach a Quranic principle called *taqiyya*. It is a form of permissible deception that allows Muslims to conceal their true intentions. When an Islamic theocracy makes promises at the negotiating table, it's important to recognize that the taqiyya principle is at work.

There is a strong chance that future peace agreements may never be honored, just as Hitler made peace with Russia through a treaty he never intended to keep, the upcoming Antichrist will sign peace deals and military pacts that he also never plans to fulfill.

As we will see in Chapter 6, the infallible prophecies of Scripture tell us that the Antichrist will make a seven-year peace treaty with Israel and break it forty-two months later. The America we cherish must not be complicit in setting the stage for this prophetic betrayal by pressuring Israel to accept false peace agreements with enemies who seek her destruction.

I take to heart what Israel's Prime Minister Benjamin Netanyahu wrote to the organization I founded, Christians United for Israel, after the October 7 attacks on Israel.

> *"Now is the hour for all civilized people that value human life and decency to stand together against the forces of evil. As we continue to mourn the many lives so violently taken, we embrace our moral obligation to safeguard our people and the common values of humanity."*

He's right, and it's especially true for America's Christians. We must stand with Israel until victory is achieved, and even after that.

The Choice Before Us

According to 1 Corinthians 10:32, the Bible recognizes three groups of people:

1. Israel: the Jewish nation chosen by God to be a special, national people, entrusted with His covenants, laws, and promises. They are considered the "natural branches" in God's plan.
2. The Nations: these are the Gentiles, all non-Jewish peoples. They are "alienated from the commonwealth of Israel."
3. The Church: A distinct entity consisting of believers in Jesus Christ. We are the "wild olive branches" grafted in.

The Jewish people are a covenantal nation. The covenants that God made with them still stand and will remain true forever. Israel has not been replaced by the

Church, as some teach. The Jewish people are a valued and chosen people. And it is God Who is the Chooser.

When Messiah comes, He will rule the earth from Jerusalem, where kings, queens, prime ministers, and presidents will bow before the Carpenter of Nazareth and declare to the world that He is the King of Kings and Lord of Lords.

America stands at a crossroads. Our national prosperity — in fact, our very survival — depends on our obedience as a nation. This isn't just a political stance, it's a Biblical position that has political consequences. The choice is ours to make. But make no mistake: the outcome of this choice belongs to God. And He has clearly outlined the framework for His decision.

Nations do not stand before God. People do.

The question is not only what will America choose.

The question is what will you choose.

The Church has a voice. The Church has a mandate. The Church has a Savior Who is coming back. The sleeping Church must wake up.

CHAPTER 5:

THE SLEEPING CHURCH MUST WAKE UP

A Call to Watch, Warn, and Stand with Israel

For Zion's sake I will not hold my peace, and for Jerusalem's sake I will not rest, until her righteousness goes forth as brightness, and her salvation as a lamp that burns.

ISAIAH 62:1

In the fall of 1943, with the Holocaust death machine operating across Nazi-occupied Europe, a young German pastor named Dietrich Bonhoeffer sat in a prison cell at Tegel Military Prison in Berlin. His crime? Resisting the Nazi regime and helping Jews escape to Switzerland. While most German churches had either embraced Hitler's ideology or remained silent, Bonhoeffer chose to speak out.

Years earlier, Bonhoeffer had penned these haunting words: "Silence in the face of evil is itself evil: God will not hold us guiltless. Not to speak is to speak. Not to act is to act."

The German church of the 1930s and 40s stands as one of history's most sobering examples of what happens when God's people become complacent. While a satanic regime systematically murdered six million Jewish men, women, and children, most of the world's Christians remained silent. Some even offered theological justification for the atrocities by promoting a teaching that claimed the Church had replaced Israel in God's plan, and that, therefore, the Jewish people no longer mattered to God. This demonic theology is called Replacement Theology, or Supersessionism. But no matter what it is called, it is heretical and evil.

Hitler had no objection to that theology, nor do modern-day antisemites. The Jewish people have always been the scapegoats.

Today, as prophetic events quicken around us and antisemitism spreads through our streets, campuses, and even some churches, we must ask ourselves a serious question. Namely, is the Church of Jesus Christ awake? Or are we sleeping through the most critical prophetic hour since Israel's rebirth in 1948?

Or are we sleeping through the most critical prophetic hour since Israel's rebirth in 1948?

Silence Is Not an Option

The prophet Isaiah shows us the way to navigate this time. In Isaiah 62:1, we read: *"For Zion's sake I will not hold my peace, and for Jerusalem's sake I will not rest, until her righteousness goes forth as brightness, and her salvation as a lamp that burns."*

Notice that the Word of God uses the names "Zion" and "Jerusalem" interchangeably here. So, we could also read this verse: "For Israel's sake, I will not keep silent. And for Jerusalem's sake, I will not hold my peace." This is not a suggestion. It is a directive, and the holy Scripture is pointing the way.

What does this command mean? It clearly states that when antisemitism rears its ugly head — whether in Congress, on college campuses, in churches, on city streets, or at the water cooler — Christians are not to stay silent. We are to speak out in defense of Israel and the Jewish people. We are to push back against the propaganda. We are to call out the lies.

We are to speak out in defense of Israel and the Jewish people. We are to push back against the propaganda. We are to call out the lies.

Why? Because antisemitism is a sin. Seeing evil and not calling it out is itself evil. Not speaking up is, in a real sense, speaking. Not acting is, in effect, acting. God will not hold us guiltless if we stand by and allow His people to be attacked.

As we've seen at various points, antisemitic incidents in America have surged in recent years, especially after October 7, 2023. Our colleges and universities have become centers of Jew-hatred. Meanwhile, powerful self-claimed Christian "influencers" are brainwashing young people to despise Israel and the Jewish community. All the while, large portions of the Church have responded with a collective shrug and a dismissive yawn.

This has to come to an end. The sleeping Church must wake up and take action.

A Debt of Gratitude

Why should Christians care about Israel and the Jewish people? The apostle Paul answers this question directly in Romans 15:27. Speaking of the responsibility of Gentile believers toward the Jewish people, Paul writes: *"For if the Gentiles have been partakers of their spiritual things, their duty is also to minister to them in material things."*

Please note the word: *duty*. Paul doesn't say it's optional. He doesn't say it's a nice thing to do if you feel like it. No. He says it is the believer's *duty* — our obligation — to bless the Jewish people in tangible, natural ways in gratitude for the spiritual riches they have given us.

What are these "spiritual things" the Jewish people have given us? Consider the following:

- They gave us the Word of God. Every word in your Bible was written by Jewish hands, with the possible exception of Luke. Every prophet, every psalmist, every apostle who penned the sacred Scriptures was Jewish.
- They gave us the patriarchs — Abraham, Isaac, and Jacob. The Bible says Abraham was a friend of God. He is the father of all who believe, making him our spiritual father.
- They gave us prophets who foretold of the coming Messiah. They provided us with the covenants and God's promises. They bestowed upon us the Shekinah Glory — the visible, tangible presence of God among His people.
- And most importantly, they gave us our Redeemer—Jesus Christ Himself.

Jesus told the Samaritan woman at the well — a person who clearly was harboring some anti-Jewish resentments: *"Salvation is of the Jews"* (John 4:22). Think about that statement. If there had been no Jewish people, there would have been no Bible, no prophets, no patriarchs, no apostles, no New Testament church, no Jesus Christ, no crucifixion, no forgiveness of sin, and no eternal life.

Are you grateful for the Bible? Are you grateful for Jesus? Then you should also be grateful to the Jewish people. It is inconsistent to value the Word and the Word made flesh (John 1:14) without thanking the Jewish people, who have endured thirty-five centuries of oppression, hatred, and death to bring the sacred Scriptures to the world.

The Lie of Replacement Theology

Tragically, churches across America are teaching the false doctrine of Replacement Theology. This destructive teaching claims that the Church has replaced Israel in God's plan — that the Covenant Maker is finished with the Jewish people and His promises to Israel no longer exist and now exclusively belong to the Church.

This doctrine is a hellish lie created to justify religious antisemitism. It must be eliminated from every pulpit in America, Europe, and the world. Consider just a few of the Biblical reasons why Replacement Theology is false.

Israel was scattered among the nations by the Roman Empire in 70 A.D., yet in May 1948, the Jewish state was miraculously reborn (Isaiah 66:8). If God replaced the Jewish people, why did He bring them out of their Gentile graves and regather them to Israel just as He promised He would? (Isaiah 60:4–9)

Why is Israel today one of the most prosperous nations on Earth? As I explored in Chapter 1, the answer is that God's covenant with Abraham remains in effect, unaltered and eternal.

God's covenant with Abraham remains in effect, unaltered and eternal.

Second, the apostle Paul directly addresses this question in Romans 11:1. After two chapters establishing God's stance on the Jewish people, Paul asks: *"Has God cast away His people?"* His answer — μὴ γένοιτο in the strongest possible Greek — is: "Certainly not!"

Then Paul expands on his answer with solid logic: *"I also am an Israelite, of the seed of Abraham, of the tribe of Benjamin."* In other words, if God is done with the

Jewish people, why is He using me? And if He's using me but not them, then God is a respecter of persons, and His Word is a lie.

Third, based on the judgment of the nations described in Matthew 25, Jesus says: *"Inasmuch as you did it to one of the least of these My brethren, you did it to Me."* (v. 40). What is the criteria on which the nations will be judged? It is how those nations treated the Jewish people. If God doesn't care about the Jewish people, why is He preparing to judge the nations based on their treatment of them?

Fourth, when Jesus returns, He will be called *"the Lion of the tribe of Judah, the Root of David"* (Revelation 5:5). Did you know that the name "Judah" is the origin of the word "Jew"? Jesus is returning as the Jewish Messiah and identifies with the Jewish people. If He has abandoned them, why is His very name associated with them in the final book of your Bible?

No, friend, the Church has not replaced Israel. We have been grafted into Israel's covenants through faith in Jesus Christ. As Paul explains in Romans 11, we are wild olive branches grafted into the cultivated olive tree. We do not support the root — the root supports us. Any theology that disconnects the Church from its Jewish roots is not just false; it leads to spiritual disaster.

Watch and Pray: The Missing Message

I've had Christians ask me: "Pastor Hagee, what difference does it make whether I believe in the rapture or not?" Oh, what a difference it makes.

If you are not seeking the coming of Christ, you won't be ready when He comes. That's not just my opinion; it's a warning directly from Jesus. In Luke 21:36, Jesus says, *"Watch therefore, and pray always that you may be counted worthy to escape all these things that will come to pass, and to stand before the Son of Man."*

To "watch" means to be expectant. You don't watch for something you're not anticipating. If you are expecting something, it's because you believe it exists. The opposite is also true. You won't be watching for it if you don't believe it. And according to Jesus, failing to watch means you will not *"be counted worthy to escape all these things that will come to pass."*

Sadly, most American churches don't preach this message. Instead, they often present a version of a social Gospel. Usually, the simple, seeker-friendly message is: "We're good. God's good. Let's all be good. Good-bye!" This is superficial preaching — lacking depth, nourishment, prophetic urgency, and a call to readiness.

Meanwhile, the signs Jesus told us to watch for are clearly visible all around us. As we saw in Chapter 3, the coalition of nations that Ezekiel predicted 2,600 years ago is forming and in place. The enemies are aligned. The stage is set. Yet much of the Church remains asleep.

Peter warned us about this. In 2 Peter 3:3–4, he writes: *"Knowing this first: that scoffers will come in the last days, walking according to their own lusts, and saying, 'Where is the promise of His coming?'"* Consider the irony here. The fact that many people today don't believe He's returning is actually proof that He's almost here.

The Bible states: *"To those who eagerly wait for Him He will appear a second time, apart from sin, for salvation"* (Hebrews 9:28). Once more, the implications for those who are not awake and watching are sobering. If you're not looking for Him, He's not coming for you. He's only coming for those who love Him and anticipate His blessed appearance.

Salt That Has Lost Its Savor

The cultural research and data analysis conducted by George Barna's organization in recent years reveal a concerning outlook for the American church. My personal view of their findings suggests that many professing Christians have adopted increasingly unchristian beliefs. Additionally, many who claim the name of Christ hold worldviews that are nearly identical to those of the surrounding pagan culture — primarily due to the widespread acceptance of "syncretism."

"Syncretism" is the fancy word researchers use — the blending of Biblical faith with pagan ideas until they become indistinguishable. Americans are building worldviews based on feelings, experiences, personal preferences, and cultural trends rather than the unchanging Word of God.

As Barna notes in his 2025 American Worldview Inventory, syncretism dominates the American landscape (embraced by 92% of adults), leading most people to believe that the goal of life is feeling good about themselves; that all faiths hold equal value; that entering God's eternal presence depends on one's personal choice; and that there are no moral absolutes to guide us.[xvii]

Child of God, this is not the faith once delivered to the saints (Jude 1:3). This is "fear of cancel culture" Christianity — a faith that has been edited to avoid offending anyone, including the forces of darkness.

Jesus warned us about this. He said: *"You are the salt of the earth; but if the salt loses its flavor, how shall it be seasoned? It is then good for nothing but to be thrown out and trampled underfoot by men"* (Matthew 5:13).

Salt preserves. Salt slows down decay and corruption. As long as the Church of Jesus Christ acts as salt in the earth, we effectively hold back the full power of evil. Every secular humanist, every Satanist, every pagan spiritual force operating in America cannot dominate as long as the Church of Jesus Christ is here doing what Jesus called us to do.

But salt that has lost its flavor is worthless. A church that refuses to speak prophetic truth, stand with Israel, confront evil, watch, and pray — such a church is on the verge of being *"thrown out and trampled underfoot."* (Matthew 5:13)

The sleeping Church must wake up.

A Practical Response

What does it mean to "wake up" and stand with Israel? I have provided an answer in this chapter. Let me summarize with five declarations:

First, it means praying. As I mentioned earlier in Chapter 2, we are commanded to pray for the peace of Jerusalem

(Psalm 122:6). When you pray for the peace of Jerusalem, you are releasing God's favor upon yourself, your family, and your nation continually. It will shake the gates of Hell and open the windows of Heaven.

Second, it involves speaking out. When antisemitism surfaces, speak up and confront those who target the Jewish people. Don't stay silent. Silence equals complicity. To the pastors across America: What is your church doing to support Israel? It matters to God now, and it will also matter at the judgment.

Third, it involves giving. Paul stated that it is our duty to support the Jewish people in their material needs. Practical acts of kindness toward God's Chosen open the door to God's blessing. The centurion in Luke 7 built a synagogue for the Jewish people, and when he needed a miracle, Jesus provided it. When you bless Israel, God will bless you.

Fourth, it means watching. Lift your heads and rejoice, for your redemption is near (Luke 21:28). Study the prophetic Scriptures. Understand the times. Recognize the signs. As the enemies align and the birth pangs grow stronger, know that God is moving according to His perfect timetable.

Fifth, it means being prepared. If Jesus were to come today, are you ready to meet Him? Is there unconfessed sin in your life? Have you made Him the Lord of your life, or are you just singing about Heaven without any real intention of going there?

The Question Before Us

The Church of Jesus Christ has two Biblical responsibilities toward Israel: to pray for the peace of Jerusalem and to comfort the Jewish people — especially now, as they are under attack from all sides and facing the worst outbreak of antisemitism since World War II. Regarding that second responsibility, God, through the prophet Isaiah, commanded: *"Comfort, yes, comfort My people!' Says your God"* (Isaiah 40:1).

I feel compelled to ask some pointed questions.

To you, the person reading this book: how have you treated the Jewish people? Remember, as I discussed in Chapter 1, Israel is God's firstborn son. They are the apple of His eye. What have you done (literally) to bless the Jewish people?

To church leaders: What steps is your church taking to bless Israel? Are you teaching your congregation about God's everlasting covenant with Abraham? Are you publicly standing with Israel during her time of need? Or are you neglecting your duty as a watchman on the wall?

Indeed, the question every believer must ask themselves in this hour is: "Am I awake, aligned, and active — or am I asleep?"

When the Church is raptured from this earth in the blink of an eye, when the trump of God sounds and the dead in Christ rise first, and when we who are alive and remain are caught up to meet the Lord in the air — churches around the world will be flooded with people who were "playing church." The lukewarm. The backslidden. The people who knew about Christ but never truly received Him as Lord of their lives. Don't be one of them.

For the first time in two thousand years, millions of Christians in America and around the world are standing with Israel. We are obeying God's Word. We are watching and praying. We lift our heads because our redemption is near.

The King is coming. The dormant Church needs to wake up.

The watchman has seen the sword coming. The trumpet has sounded. The warning has been given.

Now lift your eyes.

What comes next is not a tragedy. It is a triumph. It is the moment Heaven has been building toward since the garden of Eden.

The rapture. The tribulation. The second coming. The King returning in power and great glory.

He is coming.
Are you ready to meet Him?

CHAPTER 6:

THE KING IS COMING WITH POWER AND GLORY

The Rapture, the Tribulation, and the Return of Christ

Behold, He is coming with clouds, and every eye will see Him, even they who pierced Him. And all the tribes of the earth will mourn because of Him. Even so, Amen.

REVELATION 1:7

Do you hear it? The clock is ticking. The hands steadily, relentlessly continue to move around the face of God's celestial timepiece. And as our examination of God's prophetic clock has already revealed, the hour is oh so late.

We began with God's unchanging, unbreakable covenant with Abraham. We clearly saw the eternal significance of Jerusalem. We noted the precise alignment of enemy nations prophesied by Ezekiel. We have observed the alarming rise of hatred for Israel and the Jewish people here in America — placing our nation at a critical crossroads. We have borne witness to the urgent need for the Church to awaken while time remains.

Taken together, these signs align perfectly toward an upcoming, decisive event on Heaven's schedule: the return of the King.

The Bible clearly explains what is ahead. From Genesis to Revelation, Scripture vividly describes the end of this age as we know it and the beginning of the next. There are two comings yet to occur, two resurrections that will take place, two destinies awaiting humanity — and one returning King Who will settle all matters.

Let me state this clearly: Jesus Christ is coming back. He is literally and visibly returning to the earth. When He does, everything changes. So, let's examine the exact sequence of events that begins to unfold at a moment only the Father knows, a moment He has already set in motion.

The Taking Away of the Church

When the minute hand on God's chronometer reaches the exact moment, the first event that signals the end of this present age is what the Bible calls the "catching away" of the Church — what we usually refer to as the rapture. Please understand, this is not the second coming. The rapture is when Jesus returns to gather His Church. The second coming, which occurs seven years later, is when Jesus returns to Earth with His Church. These are two separate, glorious events.

The rapture is when Jesus returns to gather His Church.

As we noted in Chapter 3, Paul describes the rapture in vivid detail in 1 Thessalonians 4:16–17:

> *For the Lord Himself will descend from heaven with a shout, with the voice of an archangel, and with the trumpet of God. And the dead in Christ will rise first. Then we who are alive and remain shall be caught up together with them in the clouds to meet the Lord in the air.*

Notice the precision of Paul's language here. He says *"the Lord Himself"* — not an angel, not a representative, but the resurrected, glorified Christ, personally. The Bible is not sloppy about word choices. The Holy Spirit, Who inspired the writers of God's Word, chooses words with great intentionality. *"The Lord Himself"* is a double confirmation to ensure you have no doubt that this is Jesus descending from Heaven.

Here is the picture the Bible depicts: Jesus Christ, the Prince of Glory, suddenly appears in the clouds of Heaven, shining brightly like lightning flashing from east to west in a burst of dazzling white. The trumpet of God will sound — actually, this "trumpet" is Israel's shofar — announcing the arrival of royalty.

This is fitting for Jesus, Who is the Prince of Peace, the King of Kings, and the Lord of Lords. Then the voice of the archangel calls the righteous dead from their graves as they rise into the Heavens. The living believers are transformed in an instant and are caught up together with the resurrected saints to meet the Lord in the air.

This is not a new idea exclusive to the New Testament. In the Old Testament, we see clear examples of godly men who simply vanished from the earth without experiencing death. The Bible states Enoch walked with God and was not, for God took him (Genesis 5:24; Hebrews 11:5). Enoch has been in Heaven for thousands of years. The prophet Elijah was taken into Heaven in a chariot of fire (2 Kings 2:11).

And on resurrection morning, the Bible tells us that people in Jerusalem saw those who had been buried walking down the streets of the city (Matthew 27:52–53). The idea of believers being supernaturally taken from Earth to Heaven has strong Biblical support.

A Literal Event, Not an Allegory

Some who criticize the doctrine of the rapture say it is not meant to be taken literally — that it is just allegorical. But let me tell you something: the Bible is not an allegorical book. An allegory is essentially fictional, a myth. If the Bible is a myth, then I am myth-taken, myth-tified, and of all men most myth-erable — to paraphrase Saint Paul in 1 Corinthians 15:19.

The Bible should be understood literally from beginning to end. It begins with the literal creation of Heaven and Earth. God Almighty genuinely fulfilled everything He said He would do and continues to do everything He promises.

Jesus was truly born of the Virgin Mary. He was truly born in Bethlehem, Israel. He truly taught, healed the sick, and cast out demons. He truly died on the Cross and was buried in a borrowed grave. He truly rose from the dead on the third day and was seen by over 500 people in different locations, as recorded in the New Testament.

He truly rose from the dead on the third day and was seen by over 500 people in different locations, as recorded in the New Testament.

He is literally at the right hand of God the Father right now. He will literally come back with power and great glory. Every knee will literally bow before Him.

And every tongue shall literally confess that He is Lord to the glory of God the Father.

We are literally going to meet Him in the air. We are literally going to walk down streets of gold. We will literally wear a crown of life. We will literally live forever and ever, because eternal life is literally guaranteed in the Word of God.

No, there's nothing symbolic or figurative about the Bible's teachings on the rapture. The same applies to everything else the Bible says about Jesus' return.

Let me remind you what the angels told the eleven slack-jawed disciples after watching Jesus ascend into Heaven. In Acts 1:11, two angels asked: *"Men of Galilee, why do you stand gazing up into heaven? This same Jesus, who was taken up from you into heaven, will so come in like manner as you saw Him go into heaven."*

Note those three vital words: *"this same Jesus."* Once again, the Scripture clearly leaves no room for doubt. Also, notice the words *"in like manner."* What does this mean? It means, "Folks, you just saw Him leave in the same way, and you will see Him return in the same way." Jesus physically and visibly left, and He will physically and visibly return.

A Glorified Body

One of the most amazing truths about the rapture is what will happen to our physical bodies at that moment. The Bible states that when He appears to take us away, we will instantly have glorified bodies (Philippians 3:21). Consider what that means: a body free from disease, decline, and the limitations that afflict us in this fallen world.

A body free from disease, decline, and the limitations that afflict us in this fallen world.

Someone once asked me, "Is there any hope for my body?" I said, "Yes. That hope is called the resurrection of Jesus Christ." Because Jesus emerged from that tomb in Jerusalem with a glorified body, we can be sure that we, too, will have a new body when Christ appears.

Perhaps you're wondering, considering all the pretenders and false messiahs that have appeared throughout history, how we will recognize the real Jesus when He comes. Indeed, Jesus Himself warned us about this. In Matthew 24:26, He said: *"Therefore if they say to you, 'Look, He is in the desert!' do not go out; or 'Look, He is in the inner rooms!' do not believe it."*

Will it be the scars in His hands? Surgeons can create those. Miracles? The Antichrist and the False Prophet will perform miraculous signs that will deceive many. No, the proof that the real Jesus has come will be unmistakable: when our bodies leave this earth, transformed, and ascend into the Heavenlies to meet Him in the air — that is when we will know that He is the real Messiah. Only the Son of God can raise the dead and transform the living. Yes, the rapture is the first of earth's last things. So, what comes next?

Only the Son of God can raise the dead and transform the living.

The Great Tribulation

The Bible describes a seven-year period of intense suffering on earth called the tribulation, or sometimes the great tribulation. This is when God Almighty tells a world that has rejected His Son and His message: "You wanted to live without Me? Very well. I will let you see what that looks like."

The tribulation is a period during which the world will be under the rule of the Antichrist, who is also called the "son of perdition" in Scripture. "Perdition" is an Old English term meaning "a state of eternal punishment and damnation." Naturally, the one for whom the lake of fire was originally prepared was Satan himself. This means that the title "son of perdition" essentially indicates the chief son of Satan. Just as Jesus is the Son of God, the Antichrist is the son of the devil. During those seven devastating years, this satanic messiah will bring terror to the earth.

The book of Revelation describes twenty-one judgments that will cause one-third of the earth's population to die, with the seal and bowl judgments bringing additional catastrophic death and destruction. Plagues will spread across the earth. Famine will also occur, as shown by the rider on the black horse holding scales, selling a day's worth of food for a day's wages (Revelation 6:5–6). The four horsemen of the Apocalypse will bring conquest, war, famine, and death.

The book of Revelation warns that one-third of all vegetation on Earth will be destroyed. The grass and trees will suffer severe damage. The sun and moon will grow dark as nature revolts. When the moon no longer regulates the tides, typhoons and devastating floods will become common.

The gates of Hell will open, and hordes of demonic locusts will fly across the earth, stinging people for five months with the tormenting pain of a scorpion. Men will gnaw their tongues and beg God to let them die — and He will not allow it (Revelation 9:1–6). The seven seas will turn to blood. Every person with the mark of the beast will be covered with running sores.

A world war will occur, so destructive that the blood will flow to the bridles of horses for two hundred miles in the Valley of Megiddo (Revelation 14:20). This is not poetic language; it is prophetic reality.

Some critics of the rapture doctrine call it "escapism." My response? The rapture is no more escapism than divine healing is escapism from disease. Environmentalists want to escape pollution. The peace movement wants to escape war. The Bible explicitly teaches us to prepare to escape. Luke 21:36 says: *"Watch therefore, and pray always that you may be counted worthy to escape all these things that will come to pass, and to stand before the Son of Man."* Hebrews 2:3 asks: *"How shall we escape if we neglect so great a salvation?"*

Escape what? Escape the great tribulation — and we escape through the rapture of the Church.

The Rider on the White Horse

The book of Revelation is God pulling back the veil to reveal the future of the world to the Bride of Christ.

The book of Revelation is God pulling back the veil to reveal the future of the world to the Bride of Christ.

God is telling the Church: "I am the God Who knows the end from the beginning. I am in complete control of kings and kingdoms. Do not worry, because I am showing you exactly what will happen."

Revelation reveals that the Antichrist will come riding a white horse (Revelation 6:2). Some have falsely taught that this rider is Jesus Christ. The rider on the white horse in Revelation 6 is the Antichrist. He is a man — not a computer, not an organization — but a person (Daniel 8:15). He is Satan's demonic messiah (Daniel 8:24).

Paul tells us in 2 Thessalonians 2:7–8 that *"the mystery of lawlessness is already at work; only He who now restrains will do so until He is taken out of the way. And then the lawless one will be revealed, whom the Lord will consume with the breath of His mouth and destroy with the brightness of His coming."* The "He" Who restrains is the Holy Spirit, working through the Church.

The Holy Spirit came to the Church in the upper room at Pentecost, and when the Church is taken up in the rapture, the restraining influence of the Holy Spirit will be removed from the earth. Then Satan will be released to allow his Antichrist to step onto the stage of history.

The Antichrist will be a charismatic political genius. He will lead ten kings, conquer three, and lead the remaining seven into the battle of Armageddon (Daniel 7:24; Revelation 13:1). He will be a master of deception.

He will be a master of deception.

Jesus warned in Matthew 24:4: *"Take heed that no one deceives you."* If it were possible, even the elect would be deceived. He will be extremely arrogant — Daniel 8:25 (KJV) says he will *"magnify himself in his heart."* He will understand *"dark sentences"* (v. 23), meaning he will have a satanic anointing to know secret things. The Bible says he will come to power *"but not by his own power"* (Daniel 8:24) — the devil himself will anoint and empower him.

This Antichrist will establish a one-world religion. He will set up his image in Jerusalem and command the world to worship him. Those who refuse will be killed (Revelation 13:15). He will introduce the mark of the beast — a mark on the right hand or forehead — without which no one can buy or sell (Revelation 13:16–17). God's warning about this mark couldn't be clearer.

> *"If anyone worships the beast and his image, and receives his mark on his forehead or on his hand, he himself shall also drink of the wine of the wrath of God, which is poured out full strength into the cup of His indignation. He shall be tormented with fire and brimstone in the presence of the holy angels and in the presence of the Lamb."*
> (Revelation 14:9–10)

Here's the good news: the Antichrist will rise, but he will fall. His reign of terror has an expiration date. God has already written the final chapter. This leads us to the next major milestone in God's grand finale.

The Second Coming: The King of Kings Returns

Seven years after the rapture, at the end of the tribulation, Jesus Christ will physically return to Earth. This event is known as the second coming — distinct from the rapture and far more glorious.

The first time Jesus came, He was nailed to a Cross. The next time He comes, He will reign from His father David's throne in Jerusalem. It will be a literal throne in a real kingdom. The first time He came, He rode a donkey into Jerusalem. The next time He comes, He will be riding a white horse, and the armies of Heaven — including the raptured Church — will be mounted on white horses behind Him. We will thunder through the clouds of Heaven toward the battle of Armageddon and proclaim Him as King of all kings and Lord of all lords.

As I described in Chapter 2, Jesus will set His feet on the Mount of Olives, walk through the Kidron Valley, enter through the Eastern Gate of Jerusalem, and establish Himself as the Son of the Living God. The nations of the earth will bow before Him.

Zechariah 14:4 states that when His feet touch the Mount of Olives, the mountain will split in two from east to west, forming a large valley. The cemetery in front of the Golden Gate to prevent His entry will not delay Him even for a moment. The sealed gate will pose no obstacle to the Creator of the universe.

The cemetery in front of the Golden Gate to prevent His entry will not delay Him even for a moment.

From Jerusalem, He will govern according to the principles of righteousness outlined in the Word of God. The Ten Commandments will be displayed in schools and universities. They will be respected, not mocked. The Word of God will dominate from sea to shining sea and reach every nation on the face of the earth.

The Defeat of Satan and His Messiah

The most terrifying message Satan will ever hear is that Jesus Christ, the Son of David, has returned to Jerusalem. Why? Because the top priority in Heaven's plan when Jesus comes back is to cast the devil and his perverted proxies — the Antichrist and the False Prophet — into the lake of fire (Revelation 19:20; 20:10).

God Almighty will defeat the Antichrist at the battle of Armageddon and cast him alive into the lake of fire and brimstone. Satan's defeat is certain. He has been defeated by the Word, by the blood, and by the name of Jesus Christ. Jesus Christ is the Lion of the Tribe of Judah. He is the Mighty One of Israel. He is victorious over death, Hell, and the grave.

Satan's defeat is certain. He has been defeated by the Word, by the blood, and by the name of Jesus Christ.

As I mentioned in Chapter 2, the struggle for Jerusalem is ultimately a supernatural one. God the Father has pledged the city to His Son, Jesus Christ, to govern the nations during His millennial reign. Satan desires that territory for his son — the Antichrist. This cosmic battle, which has been ongoing since Genesis 1, will finally be resolved when Jesus returns. And the outcome is certain. God has already declared the victor.

A Thousand Years of Peace

After God's enemies are defeated and King Jesus takes His seat on the throne, the world will witness something it has never experienced: a thousand years of peace. This refers to the millennial kingdom mentioned in Revelation 20.

The world will witness something it has never experienced: a thousand years of peace.

During this thousand-year period, the wolf will lie down with the lamb. Men will beat their swords into plowshares and study war no more (Isaiah 2:4). The Kingdom of Christ will span the earth. Every knee shall bow, and every tongue shall confess that Jesus Christ is Lord to the glory of God the Father (Philippians 2:10–11).

I must state a blunt truth: the person who rejects Jesus Christ and His atoning blood sacrifice will not be part of that Kingdom. They cannot. Revelation 21:8 tells us plainly that *"the cowardly, unbelieving, abominable, murderers, sexually immoral, sorcerers, idolaters, and all liars shall have their part in the lake which burns with fire and brimstone, which is the second death."*

Two resurrections. Two destinies. One leads to eternal life in the presence of the King, while the other results in eternal separation from God in outer darkness. The choice each person must face is clear: Will you accept Jesus Christ as Lord and Savior, or will you risk relying on Satan's messiah?

Following that 1,000-year reign of peace, the final event unfolds in the sequence set by God's prophetic clock.

The New Jerusalem: Our Eternal Home

As I explained in Chapter 2 regarding the earthly city of Jerusalem, God has promised to create a New Jerusalem — an ultimate suburb in space, a city whose builder and maker is God (Hebrews 11:10). This will be the dwelling place of God's saints for all eternity. Once again, I must stress, this is not a metaphor. It is a literal, physical city that will descend from Heaven to earth, approximately 1,500 miles in length, width, and height.

It is described as the city where roses never fade, where the lame leap with joy, where the deaf hear, and the blind see. It is a city where there is no crying and no dying, no parting and no sorrow, for the former things have passed away (Revelation 21:4).

It is a city where there is no crying and no dying, no parting and no sorrow, for the former things have passed away.

It is a city without death or disease. It is a city where Jesus Christ dwells, for the Lamb is the light of it (Revelation 21:23). It is the city where Abraham, Isaac, and Jacob reign in mansions built by the Master Architect of the ages.

When the shofar-trump of God sounds, when the dead in Christ rise, and when the living are raptured to meet the Lord in the air — it will be the greatest moment in all of history when the Church of Jesus Christ goes home.

Are You Ready?

When I say the rapture of the Church is imminent, I mean it can happen at any time. That is not an overstatement. If anything, it is an understatement. As we saw in Chapter 3, the coalition of nations described by Ezekiel 2,600 years ago is already formed and in position. The enemies are aligned. The stage is set.

We are not waiting for some mysterious event before the prophetic clock can advance. We are simply waiting for the sound of the trumpet — when the trump of God shall sound and the dead in Christ shall rise.

We are simply waiting for the sound of the trumpet — when the trump of God shall sound and the dead in Christ shall rise.

I'm compelled to once more ask you, dear reader, are you prepared? If Jesus Christ were to come before you finish reading this book, are you ready to meet Him? Is there unconfessed sin in your life? Have you made Him the Lord of your life?

I have set before you life and death (Deuteronomy 30:19). I have set before you Heaven and Hell. I have set before you Jesus Christ, the Prince of Peace, and Satan's messiah, the Antichrist. Both are on their way. Which will you choose to serve?

The book of Revelation is the story of the Church of Jesus Christ overcoming the world, the flesh, and the devil. It is the story of the Church triumphant over death, Hell, and the grave. It is the story of the rapture of the Church leaving this broken world for mansions on high. And it is the story of our King returning in power and glory to claim His rightful throne.

> *Behold, He is coming with clouds, and every eye will see Him, even they who pierced Him. And all the tribes of the earth will mourn because of Him. Even so, Amen.* (Revelation 1:7)

The King is coming.

You have seen the covenant. You have seen the city. You have seen the enemies aligning. You have seen America at the crossroads. You have heard the call to the sleeping Church. You have watched the King prepare His return.

There is only one question left. What will you do with what you know?

The clock is striking midnight. The night is far spent. The day is at hand.

Maranatha.
Even so, come, Lord Jesus.

CHAPTER 7:

MIDNIGHT ON GOD'S PROPHETIC CLOCK

Living Ready in the Final Hour

And do this, knowing the time, that now it is high time to awake out of sleep; for now our salvation is nearer than when we first believed. The night is far spent, the day is at hand. Therefore let us cast off the works of darkness, and let us put on the armor of light.

ROMANS 13:11-12

Tick. Tick. Tick. In 1947, a group of atomic scientists created what they called the "Doomsday Clock" — a symbolic clock meant to show how close humanity is to catastrophic destruction. When the clock was first introduced, the hands were set at seven minutes to midnight, with midnight symbolizing the point of ultimate doom.

As humanity has swung between hostility and peace in the following decades, the hands of that ominous clock have moved back and forth, yet constantly reminding us that nuclear destruction could be just moments away.

God has a similar clock, and its hands never go backward. Always moving forward.

Throughout the previous chapters of this book, we have followed God's prophetic plan. We started with the unbreakable covenant God made with Abraham — a promise that made Israel His chosen nation forever. We looked at Jerusalem, the city God calls His own, the center of all prophecy, and the future throne of the returning King.

We identified the enemies now aligning exactly as Ezekiel prophesied twenty-six centuries ago. We confronted America's crossroads — a nation that must choose between blessing Israel and facing divine judgment. We issued an urgent wake-up call to the sleeping Church about her urgent responsibilities in this late hour. And in our previous chapter, we traced the magnificent sequence of events that will unfold when Jesus returns — the rapture, the tribulation, the second coming, and the glorious millennial reign.

Now, as we finish this study of God's prophetic clock, we must ask the most urgent question of all: What time is it?

The answer is clear: it's just moments from midnight on God's prophetic clock.

The answer is clear: it's just moments from midnight on God's prophetic clock.

The apostle Paul, writing under divine inspiration, declared it is *"high time to awake out of sleep"* (Romans 13:11). That phrase carries tremendous urgency. Paul wasn't speaking to unbelievers — he was writing to the Church. He was saying: "Wake up! Open your eyes! The night is far spent. The day of the Lord is at hand. Now our salvation is nearer than when we first believed."

Signs That Are Shouting

The major signs of the times are obvious — they are loudly signaling. Jesus explained what to watch for, and those signs are now clearly visible around the world. Some Bible prophecy signs are so straightforward that even a child can understand them. You don't need to be a Bible expert fluent in Hebrew, Greek, and Aramaic to see what's happening. It's very clear.

Consider what we have seen in our generation. As I mentioned in Chapter 1, Israel was reborn as a nation in May 1948—just as the Old Testament prophets predicted. Jesus said in Matthew 24:32–33: *"Now learn this parable from the fig tree: When its branch has already become tender and puts forth leaves, you know that summer is near. So, you also, when you see all these things, know that it is near — at the doors!"* Indeed, the fig tree has blossomed.

Indeed, the fig tree has blossomed.

When I was an eight-year-old child, I was listening to the radio with my father in our kitchen when the announcer interrupted the broadcast to say, "The

United Nations has recognized the State of Israel." My father looked across the table and said, "This is the most important prophetic day in the twentieth century. It validates that the Word of God is absolutely true and that the coming of the Lord Jesus Christ is going to happen soon."

Then, in 1967, Jerusalem was reunited with Israel. The Gospel of Luke tells us: *"Jerusalem will be trampled by Gentiles until the times of the Gentiles are fulfilled"* (Luke 21:24). Since 1967, Jerusalem has been under Jewish control. The prophetic clock has been ticking toward midnight ever since.

The prophetic clock has been ticking toward midnight ever since.

And then there is the knowledge explosion. In Daniel 12:4, God told the prophet: *"But you, Daniel, shut up the words, and seal the book until the time of the end; many shall run to and fro, and knowledge shall increase."* God was telling Daniel: A generation is coming whose knowledge will explode.

From the garden of Eden until the early 20th century, life remained mostly the same. People traveled by horse, just like David, Caesar, and our ancestors did. My grandparents, who were married in 1905, built churches while traveling by wagon through Texas and Oklahoma.

Think about what has happened since then. We invented the automobile, the airplane, and jets. We put a man on the moon. Technology changes so rapidly now that it can be overwhelming. Let me illustrate with this example: the cell phone.

When I was a boy and the telephone company came to install a phone in our home, it was mounted in a pine box on the wall. It was a party line — my family and two other families shared it. If you wanted to call someone long distance, you had to dial an operator who would connect you to another operator in the city you were calling, and the process usually took fifteen to twenty minutes. Today, I can call people on the other side of the world in ten seconds on this small device in my pocket. That, my friend, is the knowledge explosion.

We are that generation. We are the generation that has witnessed the knowledge explosion Daniel prophesied 2,600 years ago.

As we discussed in Chapter 3, the alliance of nations described by Ezekiel — Russia, Iran, and their allies

— has already come together. We're not waiting for some mysterious event to happen before the prophetic clock can move forward. Everything is in place.

We're not waiting for some mysterious event to happen before the prophetic clock can move forward.

Jesus said: *"When these things begin to come to pass, then look up, and lift up your heads; for your redemption draweth nigh"* (Luke 21:28, KJV). Obviously, you lift your head because you're searching for someone in the sky. In the clouds. That person we're meant to be looking upward for is Jesus Christ, the King of Kings and Lord of Lords.

As I mentioned in Chapter 5, the very fact that scoffers are asking, "Where is the sign of His coming?" is itself a sign. Peter warned that in the last days, skeptics would mock the promise of Christ's return (2 Peter 3:3–4).

From Information to Intercession

Throughout this book, I have shared essential information with you. But information without application is merely education. God does not reveal His prophetic plan just to satisfy our curiosity. He reveals it so that we will act.

My goal here is not to fill your head, but to get you on your knees. It's time to move from knowledge to intercession.

The prophet Daniel received extraordinary revelation about the end times. When he saw these visions, he didn't just sit back in idle fascination. The Bible tells us Daniel set his *"face toward the Lord God to make request by prayer and supplications, with fasting, sackcloth, and ashes"* (Daniel 9:3). Daniel's response to prophetic revelation was passionate, persistent prayer.

Daniel's example influenced the design of the church I have the privilege to pastor. The pulpit of Cornerstone Church and our front doors face east toward Jerusalem. The twelve doors of our sanctuary represent the twelve tribes of Israel. Daniel prayed with his windows open toward Jerusalem three times every day. Is your prayer life that consistent?

As I mentioned earlier in Chapter 2, we are commanded to pray for the peace of Jerusalem (Psalm 122:6).

When you pray for the peace of Jerusalem, you shake the gates of Hell and open the windows of Heaven. You release God's favor upon yourself, your family, and your nation continually. You align yourself with what God is passionate about (Zechariah 8:2) — and when you align your life with God's heart, you step into His purposes for the world and your life.

When you pray for the peace of Jerusalem, you shake the gates of Hell and open the windows of Heaven.

Prayer is the key to unlocking God's supernatural power in your life, marriage, business, finances, mind, and church. Let me point you to one of the most powerful verses in the Bible — if you truly believe it. Take hold of this promise from Jesus: *"Therefore I tell you, whatever you ask for in prayer, believe that you have received it, and it will be yours"* (Mark 11:24, NIV).

We are living through a historic moment, a time when almost everything that can be shaken is being shaken. Oh, how desperately we need Heavenly power right now. We need an army of intercessors who believe those words of the Savior. Why? Because the greatest need in America is to see the Lord's power manifested in the Church. We must be conduits of that power, carriers of that power, and releasers of God's power.

We are living through a historic moment, a time when almost everything that can be shaken is being shaken.

Watchmen on the Wall

God is seeking watchmen — individuals who will stand their post on the wall and refuse to stay silent.

> *I have set watchmen on your walls, O Jerusalem; they shall never hold their peace day or night. You who make mention of the LORD, do not keep silent, and give Him no rest till He establishes and till He makes Jerusalem a praise in the earth.* (Isaiah 62:6–7)

God loves Jerusalem deeply. He desires watchmen on her walls — intercessors who will pray continually for His purposes to be fulfilled. But the role of a watchman goes beyond interceding. A watchman is also a warrior who warns of impending danger.

A watchman is also a warrior who warns of impending danger.

In Ezekiel 33, God made the prophet a watchman for the house of Israel. The watchman's job was simple. When he saw the sword — an invading army ready to destroy — approaching the land, he was to blow the trumpet and warn the people. If he blew the trumpet and they ignored the warning, their blood would be on their own heads. But if the watchman saw the sword coming and did not blow the trumpet — if he failed to warn the people — their blood would be on the watchman's hands (Ezekiel 33:1–6).

This is a serious responsibility. Recognizing evil and not calling it evil is, in itself, evil. Staying silent, as I mentioned in Chapter 5, is still speaking. Choosing not to act is, in effect, acting. God will not consider us innocent if we stand silent while the prophetic clock strikes midnight.

You are called to be a watchman in your home, your church, and your nation. Will you answer that call?

You are called to be a watchman in your home, your church, and your nation. Will you answer that call?

The Five Roles of a Watchman

What does it mean to be a watchman at this late hour? Let me give you five concrete actions.

First and most obviously, watchmen *watch*. This act is fundamental. Jesus repeatedly commanded His disciples to "watch." To stay alert, pay attention to the signs, and understand the times.

> *"Watch therefore, and pray always that you may be counted worthy to escape all these things that will come to pass, and to stand before the Son of Man"* (Luke 21:36).

"Watch and pray," Jesus said — because when you watch, you are expecting. If you are expecting, you are believing. And if you are watching and believing, you will be worthy to escape those things that are coming on the earth.

This warning is so urgent and important that I must repeat it. The person who is not watching is not expecting. The person who is not expecting is not believing. And the person who is not believing is not going with Jesus when He comes.

The person who is not watching is not expecting. The person who is not expecting is not believing. And the person who is not believing is not going with Jesus when He comes.

Second, watchmen *pray*. Prayer is the watchman's main weapon. It makes the impossible possible. It unleashes God's supernatural power into earthly situations. Do you want God's prosperity to fill your life? Pray for the peace of Jerusalem. It will bring God's blessing and favor — a prosperity no enemy of God can stop or reduce.

It will bring God's blessing and favor — a prosperity no enemy of God can stop or reduce.

Third, watchmen *alert others*. When antisemitism surfaces, speak out and confront those who attack the Jewish people. When you hear the lies of Replacement Theology, speak the truth. When the culture mocks the promise of Christ's return, stand firm on the Word of God. Don't remain silent. Silence equals complicity. Those tormenting Israel should understand that God's judgment is approaching them. God is merciful, but when boundaries are crossed, the only thing that matches His love is His wrath.

Fourth, watchmen *bless*. As we established in Chapter 1, God's promise to Abraham still stands: *"I will bless those who bless you, and I will curse him who curses you"* (Genesis 12:3). What are you doing—tangibly, practically—to bless the Jewish people? Recall Paul's words I have already brought to your attention: *"If the Gentiles have been partakers of their spiritual things, their duty is also to minister to them in material things"* (Romans 15:27). This is not optional. It is your duty.

Connect your life to what God is doing in Israel, Jerusalem, and among the Jewish people. When our church and ministry began supporting Israel and the Jewish people, we entered into God's blessings in powerful and profound ways. We have watched with awe as God has abundantly blessed our efforts to bless His land, His city, and His people.

Fifth, watchmen *stay ready*. If Jesus were to come today, are you prepared to meet Him? Have you made Him the Lord of your life?

The Hope Before Us

I want to be very clear about something: unlike the message behind the atomic scientists' "Doomsday Clock," this message is not a message of doom. It is a message of glorious hope.

It is a message of glorious hope.

Yes, the prophetic clock is nearing midnight. Yes, Israel's enemies are aligning. Yes, America stands at a crossroads. Yes, the Church must wake up. But for the child of God, these are not reasons to fear — they are reasons to rejoice!

Hope brings a joy that the world cannot give or take away. It creates a song that echoes in the midnight hour — like the song Paul and Silas sang in the jail at Philippi after they had been beaten bloody by Roman rods for preaching the Gospel of Jesus Christ. Hope is faith reaching out in the darkness, knowing the God we serve never fails. Saint Paul said: *"Rejoice in hope of the glory of God"* (Romans 5:2).

Never underestimate the power of hope. Hope enables you to believe the unbelievable, endure the unbearable, and accomplish the impossible. When you feel tempted to focus on all the bad things happening in the world, remember that God has given us a very special gift to help us through life's storms — the power of hope. There comes a moment when you must declare that the era of fear is over. Now is the time for hope.

There comes a moment when you must declare that the era of fear is over. Now is the time for hope.

As I described in Chapter 6, the book of Revelation tells the story of the Church of Jesus Christ overcoming the world, the flesh, and the devil. It highlights the Church's victory over death, Hell, and the grave. It narrates the rapture of the Church, leaving this broken world for mansions on high. And it depicts our King returning in power and glory to claim His rightful throne.

The race is nearly over, and we are giving it our all. Our departure from this broken world is very near. The same Jesus Who defeated death on a bloodstained hill called Calvary is returning — with power and great glory in the clouds of Heaven. He will reign from Jerusalem, and there will be no end to His Kingdom.

The same Jesus Who defeated death on a bloodstained hill called Calvary is returning — with power and great glory in the clouds of Heaven.

A Final Word

It's possible that you are simply not ready to meet Jesus if He were to come today. Maybe there is unconfessed sin in your life. Perhaps there are things you have done that you know are wrong. I am not here to judge you. All I am trying to do is warn you: You are out of time. Your loved ones are out of time.

The good news is, all you need to do to receive eternal life is to repent, confess your sins, and make Jesus Lord. Then you will find your name in the Lamb's Book of Life. What do you get for that? The privilege to walk the streets of gold forever, to live in a mansion of beauty and splendor with no thirty-year mortgage, to dwell in a world far beyond anything you could ever imagine — because Jesus has paid it all. It is all yours.

All you need to do is allow His precious blood to cleanse you and prepare you for the greatest adventure the world has ever known. I'm talking about the moment when we will see the King and stand in His presence.

Throughout this book, we have tracked the hands of God's prophetic clock as they steadily approach midnight. We have identified seven signs that every believer needs to understand about Israel and the end times:

- The covenant God made with Abraham is unbreakable.
- Jerusalem is the city God calls His own.
- The enemies of Israel are aligning exactly as Ezekiel prophesied.
- America stands at a crossroads that will determine its prophetic destiny.
- The sleeping Church must wake up.
- The King is coming with power and glory.
- Midnight on God's prophetic clock is now.

Now you can see that the clock has struck midnight. It is time to stay alert. The signs are increasing. The King is on the move.

Let us cast off the works of darkness and put on the armor of light. Let us watch and pray. Let us bless Israel and stand with the Jewish people. Let us proclaim the truth without apology or fear.

For now, our salvation is nearer than when we first believed.

Maranatha. Even so, come, Lord Jesus.

Let us cast off the works of darkness and put on the armor of light. Let us watch and pray. Let us bless Israel and stand with the Jewish people. Let us proclaim the truth without apology or fear.

ENDNOTES

i. International Christian Concern, *2025 Global Persecution Index: Executive Summary* (Washington, DC: International Christian Concern, January 3, 2025), 1, https://persecution.org/gpi/

ii. Open Doors, World Watch List 2025 (Open Doors International, 2025), https://www.opendoors.org/en-US/persecution/countries

iii. Over 7,000 Nigerian Christians Killed Since January, Watchdog Says," World News Group, August 14, 2025, https://wng.org/sift/over-7-000-nigerian-christians-killed-since-january-watchdog-says-1755194642

iv. World Zionist Organization and Jewish Agency for Israel, *Antisemitism General Review and Summary Report for 2024* (Jerusalem: World Zionist Organization, January 2025), https://www.wzo.org.il/sub/combatting-antisemitism/antisemitism_2024/en

v. European Union Agency for Fundamental Rights. "Jews in Europe Still Face High Levels of Antisemitism." News release, July 4, 2024. https://fra.europa.eu/en/news/2024/jews-europe-still-face-high-levels-antisemitism

vi. Combat Antisemitism Movement, *Echoes of the Past and a Warning for the Present: The Stark Reality of Record-Breaking Antisemitism in 2024* (New York: Combat Antisemitism Movement, April 30, 2025), https://combatantisemitism.org/studies-reports/

vii. Strong's Greek: 602. ἀποκάλυψις (apokalupsis) — Revelation, unveiling, disclosure," Bible Hub, https://biblehub.com/greek/602.htm

viii. Saeb Erekat, quoted in "Trump Ignores Warnings with 'Reckless Jerusalem Move,' *Al Jazeera*, December 7, 2017, https://www.aljazeera.com/news/2017/12/7/trump-ignores-warnings-with-reckless-jerusalem-move

ix. Anti-Defamation League, "Audit of Antisemitic Incidents 2024," April 22, 2025, https://www.adl.org/resources/report/audit-antisemitic-incidents-2024

x. Luke Tress, "NYC Jews Targeted in Hate Crimes More Than All Other Groups Combined in 2025 — NYPD," Times of Israel, January 7, 2026, https://www.timesofisrael.com/nyc-jews-targeted-in-hate-crimes-more-than-all-other-groups-combined-in-2025-nypd/

xi. Sarah Moskowitz, Danielle Greyman-Kennard, James Genn, and Reuters, "Suspect Charged with Murder in Shooting Deaths of Two Israel Embassy Workers," The Jerusalem Post, May 22, 2025, https://www.jpost.com/breaking-news/article-854979

xii. "82-Year-Old Woman Dies from Injuries Suffered in Boulder Attack," NBC News, June 30, 2025, https://www.nbcnews.com/news/us-news/82-year-old-woman-dies-colorado-attack-israeli-hostage-advocates-rcna216052

xiii. "Suspect Arrested After Mass Shooting Threat That Closed Texas Jewish Community Center," Jewish Telegraphic Agency, June 20, 2025, https://www.jta.org/2025/06/20/united-states/suspect-arrested-after-mass-shooting-threat-that-closed-texas-jewish-community-center

xiv. "At Least 15 Dead, Including Israeli, Dozens Wounded in Bondi Beach Hanukkah Event Massacre," Jerusalem Post, December 15, 2025, https://www.jpost.com/diaspora/article-880251

xv. Lauren Fichten, "Mississippi Synagogue Arson Suspect Said 'He Finally Got Them' After Starting Blaze, FBI Complaint Says," CBS News, January 12, 2026, https://www.cbsnews.com/news/mississippi-synagogue-arsonist-jewish-ties-fbi-complaint/

xvi. Ron E. Hassner, "From Which River to Which Sea?" Wall Street Journal, December 5, 2023, https://www.wsj.com/opinion/from-which-river-to-which-sea-anti-israel-protests-college-student-ignorance-a682463b

xvii. George Barna, "American Worldview Inventory 2025: Report 1 – Most Americans Believe in a Supreme Power, But Not the God of the Bible," Cultural Research Center at Arizona Christian University, February 18, 2025, https://www.arizonachristian.edu/wp-content/uploads/2025/02/CRC-Release-AWVI-1-Feb-18-2025-Final.pdf

NOTES

NOTES

NOTES

NOTES

ABOUT THE AUTHOR

John Hagee is the founder and senior pastor of Cornerstone Church in San Antonio, Texas, a nondenominational evangelical church with more than 22,000 active members. He is the author of more than 80 books, including several *New York Times* bestsellers, his latest being *Earth's Last Empire: The Final Game of Thrones*. Pastor Hagee is the founder and chairman of Christians United for Israel (CUFI), with over 10 million members. Hagee Ministries reaches millions worldwide through its television program, provides refuge and care to mothers and babies through the Sanctuary of Hope, and steadfastly supports Israel and the Jewish people in alignment with God's mandate to believers.

ENGAGE WITH PASTOR JOHN HAGEE ONLINE:

Hagee Ministries: jhm.org

Facebook: HageeMinistries

X: PastorJohnHagee | HageeMinistries

Instagram: PastorJohnHagee | HageeMinistries

Amazon Author Page: Find other books by Pastor John Hagee and engage further by leaving a review to encourage other readers.